MANEUVERING BETWEEN
THE HEADLINES

MANEUVERING BETWEEN THE HEADLINES

AN AMERICAN LIVES THROUGH THE INTIFADA

by Helen Schary Motro

To Loraine —
Friendship reconnected
Best regards,
Helen

Other Press • New York

The author gratefully acknowledges Karen Alkalay-Gut for permission to reprint her poem, "Almost."

Production Editor: Robert D. Hack
Text design: Kaoru Tamura
This book was set in Janson Text by Alpha Graphics of Pittsfield, NH.

10 9 8 7 6 5 4 3 2 1

Library of Congress Cataloging-in-Publication Data

Motro, Helen Schary.
    Maneuvering between the headlines : an American lives through the Intifada / by Helen Schary Motro.
        p. cm.
    ISBN 1-59051-159-X (hardcover : alk. paper) 1. Al-Aqsa Intifada, 2000–Influence. 2. Al-Aqsa Intifada, 2000–Psychological aspects. 3. Al-Aqsa Intifada, 2000–Social aspects. 4. Israel–Social conditions. 5. Jews, American–Israel–Biography. 6. Motro, Helen Schary. I. Title.
    DS119.765.M67 2005
    956.9405'4–dc22

                                                            2004020948

For my mother, Ola Schary,
whose gentleness brings dignity to every human being

TABLE OF CONTENTS

Chapter One *No Balm in Gilead*

The lobby of the Tel Aviv University Faculty of Law is filled with constant commotion. Students rush to class with books in arm; others on the couches laugh, read, or wait for their friends. Sometimes couples put their arms around each other and their heads close.

As befits law students, they seem to be always talking: chattering in fast Hebrew slang about what to expect on an upcoming exam, about a professor whose assignments are too long, or about a job interview they hope to land. Not infrequently I overhear clusters of students with the same expressions speaking a language I do not understand: Arabic.

It inevitably lifts my middle-aged spirits to pass through the lobby on the way to the course I teach.

When I was young I used to hear my friends make distinctions among our classmates' looks: between the ungainly and the over-weight, between the ones with noses too long, eyes too small, or hair too frizzy. Now, as if magically, all the young people have become beautiful.

The room buzzes with their vitality—their clear gaze and fast gait belying an unthinking confidence that the path of life lies long before them.

The lobby is a hub of activity, leading from the library and the cafeteria at one end to the staircase toward the classrooms at the other. A hodgepodge of notices tacked up on bulletin boards list job offers, apartment shares, theater festivals, opportunities for study abroad. Sometimes there are petitions to sign, leaflets to pick up, or desks set up by law firms recruiting students for jobs.

But isolated on one wall, as in every other Israeli educational institution, are mounted a series of mute photographs. In block letters above them is one stark phrase: "In Memoriam." Each of the nineteen frames bore the formal black-and-white image of an alumnus who perished as a result of the Arab–Israeli conflict. One died in the 1967 Six-Day War, nine in the Yom Kippur War of 1973, two in a helicopter disaster, one in a 1977 bus hijacking, two in Lebanon, and four of unspecified causes during their army service.

I always passed by the somber display without paying much attention. Then one afternoon my eye caught a new flash of color mounted in the very center of the wall: the only photograph in vivid color, the only one where the subject smiles brilliantly out at the camera, and the only one of a woman.

The marker beneath reads: "Ilanit Peled, graduate of the law faculty, born December 16, 1969. Killed in the terror attack in the Tel Aviv bus station, January 5, 2003." Now there are twenty photographs.

Ilanit Peled was a name I hadn't recognized or paid attention to the night of that winter bombing when the casualties were announced. The week before her death, I learned, she had completed with distinction her master's in law. Death caught her as she walked through the station on her way home from work, changing from one bus to another.

So just a few months earlier, it appears, Peled, with those gleaming eyes I saw in the photograph, with her chestnut hair, wide smile, and red sweater, had been one among the beautiful young people passing by me in the same lobby where her memorial portrait now hangs static and forever immobile. Since then I've started to wonder how many of my students use the public bus to reach my class.

My mind turns back to the beginning of this bad dream.

For someone from the northeastern United States, it is hard to get used to the fact that Israel in October is still high summer. The temperature is in the 80s and the sea inviting. We wear sandals, sleeveless shirts, and sunblock.

October 1, 2000, was no exception. If we hadn't turned on the radio, it would have seemed that all's well with the world. But the newspaper waiting on my doorstep that morning changed not only my life, but the lives of all Jews and Arabs living in this unhappy universe we call the Middle East.

For on September 30, 2000, a journalist caught live on film the shooting of a 12-year-old Palestinian boy as he cowered beside his father against a wall in Gaza. The next day the photograph of the boy's killing and the wounding of his father was featured on the front page of newspapers worldwide to stun readers around the globe. The boy, Mohammed al-Durrah, has become an icon for the Intifada, the Palestinian uprising against Israeli occupation that erupted that week, and his father a showcase of suffering around the Arab world.

If Mohammed al-Durrah had been killed today, the world would no longer have stood still in shock at his photograph. We have all become inured to killing. The intentional murders, the suicide bombings, the killing through oversight, the collateral damage from use of excessive force—all have become our bitter daily bread.

On September 30, 2002, two years to the day that Mohammed was killed, two Palestinian boys were shot dead by Israeli gunfire in the West Bank city of Nablus. Both had been involved with other children throwing rocks at Israeli tanks besieging the Arab town. A doctor at the Nablus hospital said a 10-year-old had been shot in the back of his head. A 22-year-old Israeli soldier was killed in Nablus that day by a Palestinian sniper bullet.

These deaths coincided with the day Amnesty International issued a report that cited more than 250 Palestinian children and seventy-two Israeli children killed since the outbreak of the Intifada. In addition, the report said, 7,000 Palestinian children and several hundred Israeli children had been wounded.

By 2002 the world had become used to children dying in the Mideast. The killings that took place on the second anniversary of the Intifada were reported by the world press on the inside pages of newspapers. There were no photographs of the victims.

I am an American who moved to Israel with my family in the late 1970s, moved back and forth again, and have been here since the mid-80s. A lawyer by education, I can precisely date the start of my second career as a writer. It began during the long tense days of the first Gulf War in 1991. While waiting for the sirens announcing Iraqi missile attacks, which always began after dark, sitting down to write was the way I coped with my fear.

My husband, a cardiologist whom I met in New York while he was doing his medical specialization, is a native Israeli. We have three daughters. Two are grown, and the youngest is a high school student. Growing up straddling both continents, they often asked themselves, "Are we American or are we Israeli?"

I, who brought them here and have spent so much of my adult life in Israel, still maintain the somewhat skewed attitude of an outsider, of someone not quite integrated into the interstices of the society. And so I am perceived by so many Israeli acquaintances. I see in their eyes they don't believe I *really* understand. I pick up on things that they let pass, and read differently some of the things before us both. In the face of injustices, I am always tempted to blurt out a phrase with no local recourse: "They can't do that—it's unconstitutional!"

Before she met me, my friend Bobbi in the United States heard of me from my daughter.

"My mom is an American," my daughter said.

"Oh no, she must be one of those crazy American rightists in Israel!" Bobbi's reaction mimicked what many first assume. But, to Bobbi's relief, I didn't fit the profile of the hard-line American settler living in the occupied territories, or supporting them. Yet, contrary to the impression one might get from media coverage, many Americans who have moved to Israel form the backbone of the peace movement. I am far from any activism, but I am with them in my sympathies and in my writing.

Like many who seek to transplant their lives, I've often felt like an exile in the Promised Land. Having arrived on a mix of romanticism and Second Generation Holocaust shock, I looked around me at the State of Israel the eve of its fiftieth anniversary in 1998 and observed that at 50 I was overweight and so was the State of Israel.

"She'll be another Golda Meir," our cousin, the rabbi, predicted, peering into my crib in New York in 1948. But just as I turned out far less than a Golda Meir, Israel has fallen short as well.

Everything in Israel is predicated upon its existential dilemma: that the Jewish homeland chose to define itself as a parochial nation-state that contributed to a half-century of violence.

For Israel's tenth anniversary I drew a picture in my Hebrew school class: children in blue shorts and white shirts dancing among the wild-flowers, wreaths upon their heads. It was the accepted cliché: the utopian paradise, the eternal underdog, the naive but cultured pioneer. Idealistic immigrants-turned-farmers came home after a day of physical labor to play chamber music and discuss philosophy. The rebirth of Israel, rising in the ashes of the Holocaust like a phoenix, was a miracle almost too good to be true.

But even before the Intifada, the myth was exploded by the Palestinian detainees held in administrative detention without trial and by the dominance of Israeli military industries in the international arms market.

In the decades I lived here I saw the nation redefining itself from an egalitarian socialist model to megacapitalism. Like vodka, business mixes with everything. Venture capital is the name of the game. Prestige is a master's degree in business administration. The magical seas of citrus groves are being uprooted to be turned into construction projects and tacky malls. New planned neighborhoods with identical white cottages subconsciously memorialize in the street names the nature they have plowed under: Lily of the Valley Road, Daffodil Way.

And while the gap between rich and poor expands, immigrant laborers pay exorbitant rents for windowless hovels. Tel Aviv boasts branches of Timberland, Donna Karen, Godiva, and Ralph Lauren. Even Jaguars have arrived. Ideology is dead, and the golden calf shimmers like a mirage over the horizon. One does not have to go as far as the rivers of Babylon to lament the lost Zion.

It was said that Israelis were like a cactus fruit called sabra—prickly on the outside and sweet within. Sabra was proudly adopted as their nickname by the native-born. There was to be no cloying veneer of hypocrisy, as had existed among the sycophants of the Diaspora. But the sabra's sweet interior has shrunk: over the decades Israelis have become shell-shocked by calamities, by the loss of innocent life and by killer competition for a slice of a very finite pie. Road rage is notorious, intrafamily violence is exploding, verbal abuse spills over into the physical.

Schools and public life are filled with testimonials to the fallen of the wars, yet the electorate freely voted into power a government that perpetuates force over words.

At 20 I was listening to Israeli folk songs in my college dorm, and Israel was entering its greatest watershed: the Six-Day War. By 30 I was sunning myself and my kids on the beaches near Tel Aviv, and Israel was scrambling with inflation deep into the double digits. In my 40s I was huddled with a gas mask in a room ludicrously sealed with cellophane, stuffing wet towels under the door cracks; the country was gearing up for the high-tech revolution. In my 50s I have calmed down. I wish that so too would my twin sister, the State of Israel. For there is no balm in Gilead.

Yet in my life I too am immersed in the great historical experiment known as the modern State of Israel. For all its deficiencies, I still view Israel as a miracle. There are so many instances of great humanism, great culture, and great vision.

The course of the Intifada has put my enthusiasm and my commitment to the test. How Israel chooses to deal with the Arab–Israeli dilemma, whether it will side with the great Jewish tradition of justice and righteousness, or whether it will choose the path of jingoism and militarism, raises the ultimate question: At what price the Jewish state?

I and many others fervently desire Israel to become Athens. Yet events of the last few years seem to bring it closer and closer to a paradigm of Sparta.

As I sit in my home in a Tel Aviv suburb and look out my window at the ribbon of turquoise Mediterranean in the distance beyond the green curtain of hibiscus and palm trees in my garden, the river of innocent blood seems like news from another world. Living in my town it's hard to know anything was amiss.

On the third anniversary of the start of the Intifada I received a reminder postcard from the town veterinarian. So on the following Tuesday I joined the line in front of the town hall. Beside me were a little girl with a golden retriever, a man with a collie, and a woman with a dachshund. I had my dog on her leash, the mutt that my daughter had been given by construction workers who found her five years before and that had greeted me as a fait accompli when I got home that evening. Upon a makeshift examining table the town vet administered the annual rabies shot to all the pets in town.

"Your dog gets a discount," the vet told me happily. "She is spayed."

The kindergarten opened its year with its new crop of toddlers. The municipal auditorium began its performance season with theater and

Mozart. With fall approaching the bubble would soon be put up over the town pool, to be taken down again in April.

But the normality is almost an affront. We know that not far away Palestinians have been living for months under curfew, having to go through humiliating roadblocks even on the way to deliver a baby in the hospital. Their trees have been chopped down, their houses destroyed, their livelihoods taken away. And in Israel people are afraid, and with good reason, to walk down the streets of the capital city, to enter a supermarket, to board a train.

My daughter grows taller, she moves up from middle to high school, writes essays about the Rosetta Stone, furrows her brow over isosceles triangles, races to the computer to chat with her friends, never misses her teenage soap opera on television, and swims six days a week on the swim team. Her life seems normal, but in fact it is skewed as well. Unlike a 16-year-old in the United States, she never takes the public bus. I would not let her, for fear she would be caught on the very bus blown to smithereens, the charred body parts of the passengers strewn on the roadside. She begs me to go to the mall to window-shop for clothes or go to a movie. Hearing that, my heart flies up to my throat, picturing the suicide bombers who blew themselves up outside mall entrances.

I recall 5-year-old Sasha, newly arrived from Russia, who was badly burned with his mother outside a mall in Netanya, and whose young father was killed. I remember the three teenage girls among the twenty-two victims who died near the Tel Aviv mall when they went from their country home into town for a holiday visit. But my daughter is insistent. "No bombs have gone off in Herzliya" she used to tell me adamantly, her teenage logic infallible in her own mind. But that's an argument she can't use anymore. Since then Herzliya too has joined the long list of attacks.

In 2004 all the law students in my class prepared oral presentations on legislation of their choice, ranging from copyright protection to securities regulation, from estate tax to patent law. One student chose as his topic England's Children Act, a law implementing child welfare, support, and protection.

A few days before his presentation was scheduled I received an e-mail from him: "Hello Mrs. Motro, I just wanted to let you know that unfortunately I was called to reserve service from March 1 until March 20 in the Gaza Strip. I really hope that it will be much shorter."

The attitude of people living in Israel toward the young people serving in the army is a complicated one. Even those who, like me, categorically oppose Israeli occupation of Palestinian territories feel a mixture of solicitude and worry about every soldier sent to serve in potentially dangerous locations. We may admire those who through conviction refuse military service in the occupied territories, but this does not detract from our appreciation of the soldiers who do go when called to join the several thousand Israeli soldiers stationed in Gaza. We often feel resentment too that these young people must risk—and sometimes lose—their lives to defend settlers or to take part in military operations that they might very well oppose.

A shiver of fear runs through us when we hear that someone we know is called up for duty in Gaza. It was this shiver of fear I felt when I read my student's message. In 2003 eighteen Israeli soldiers were killed in Gaza, including two 19-year-old women murdered in their sleep during a nighttime raid.

Like most others here, I am in the compulsive habit of listening to the radio news almost hourly. And as I listened to the news reports, it was my student I was thinking of.

Was he present at the Erez checkpoint on March 6 in Gaza when Palestinian vehicles disguised as Israeli jeeps loaded with explosives tried to infiltrate? There were no Israeli casualties, although in the explosions and ensuing fighting six Palestinians were killed.

More disturbing and complex were my feelings toward the events of the following day. On March 7, 2004, Israeli troops made a predawn attack on the crowded refugee camp of Nuseirat in the heart of Gaza in search of Hamas militants. Fighting spread to the nearby Al Bureij camp. As Israeli tanks and armored personnel carriers rolled through the streets and helicopters fired from above, hundreds of civilians poured into the streets to join the fray. Ten armed members of extremist organizations were killed—but so were three children under 16. The youngest was 9 years old.

I wondered if my gentle student took part in these incidents. Was he manning one of the attacking tanks? Did he pull a trigger? I hoped with all my heart that he was in some other location, maintaining equipment, doing administrative tasks, guarding a base—anything.

Not only did I fear for his physical safety, but for his moral and emotional safety, too. I did not want him to live with the memories of watching explosive-riddled cars heading to attack him in a guard post, or to have to make his peace with being part of a military force involved in the deaths of innocent civilians.

I do not know any of my students' ranks or jobs in the army, nor their political views, but I believe that they bear no blame for policies or their implementation. Blame belongs to all those who do not rise up and cry out against complacency and stalemate, who do not demand an initiative toward peace that refuses to be deterred or derailed.

My student returned to my classroom safe, smiling, and even tanned. When I inquired how it had been, he brushed off my question, saying he had been patrolling a beach. But, I wondered, when he presented his speech about the rights of minors, was he remembering other children he had just seen, children not lucky enough to be protected by any Children Act?

Often my students disappear for a week or two. Upon return they come up to me, explaining their absence by extracting from their wallets a crumpled piece of paper—their call-up order, stamped with an official triangle. I have come to look at it as the Israeli doctor's note.

A few months later into that semester, on May 11, 2004, six soldiers were killed in Gaza while engaged in a search to destroy factories producing rockets shot at Israeli settlements in Gaza as well as across the border into the "real" Israel. Their armored personnel carrier laden with explosives was blown to bits, its remains and theirs scattered over a radius hundreds of yards wide.

Palestinians were shown on television displaying their body parts. A horrified cry arose in Israel. As soldiers made a house-to-house search for human remains, debate raged in Israel about whether it was right to jeopardize more lives for this purpose.

When I began my lesson that day I silently counted heads, relieved to see each and every one of my students amble in.

On my way home I heard that another five soldiers had met an identical death. The television news showed soldiers sifting through the sand on their hands and knees, again searching for body parts.

Whereas one of the soldier's mothers said of her son, "I knew why he was there and cannot say what he did was a mistake," another father said in outrage, "I have a land, I have a people, I have an army—but I don't have a state." Then, in slurred speech, he mumbled, "I cannot imagine how I can live without him." One of the five was an Israeli Bedouin Arab, who also serve in the Israeli military. His father declared, "I hope he will be the last soldier to die." Forty-eight hours later two more were killed. The news was dominated by funerals.

Israel was in an uproar. The first page of the mass-circulation newspaper *Maariv* printed telephone survey results citing 79 percent of Israelis favoring withdrawal from Gaza. That weekend 150,000 converged on Tel Aviv for the first major peace rally in years. By the next month Israeli news was dominated by controversy about dismantling the settlements in Gaza—how, where, when, and still "if"?

Nothing is the same in Israel. The high hopes with which I and others moved here from the West have dissipated. Strife and killing seem to await us. The country has become a bitter cycle of Palestinian terror attacks, Israeli reprisals, more attacks, heavier reprisals. The threshold of violence has risen. The death of a child no longer makes headlines. We have become inured to death, hardened to tragedy, and despairing of living to see an early end to the catastrophe that seemingly fell into our laps out of the sky.

Unlike many others who have turned in disgust and despair away from the vision of peace, I still ludicrously call myself a peacenik. But what have I accomplished by attending scraggly peace marches or buying olive oil smuggled out of Palestinian villages to try to help them keep up their income? Even the dozens of commentary articles I have written, like the call to Palestinian and Jewish women to find roots in their common suffering and ally with one another on International Women's Day, speak only to those who already agree with my opinion. Others respond by writing outraged letters to the editor, calling me at best deluded liberal and at worst unprintable epithets.

Our crisis used to feel extraordinary. For months we were stunned and aghast. Instead of morning traffic updates, the radio reported roads closed because of rioting and bombs. At first normal life seemed too trivial to think about. Gradually we resumed our daily occupations and concerns, but felt guilty about them. When asked how we were, we were uncertain how to respond: "Well, OK, except for the Situation." We felt we had to mention it, the Situation, the catch-all euphemism for the inferno of hatred consuming our region since the fall of 2000. To overlook the Situation even in the most routine conversation seemed a sacrilege.

Now we have reached a stage of resignation, powerlessness, and lassitude. We anticipate that people will die, and only hope it happens less frequently, and not near us. We don't believe that even those of good faith can tip the balance, and we wonder if coexistence without bloodshed will ever again seem within our grasp. The Situation has gone from the acute to the chronic. It is our ugly second skin, a malady we have learned to live with, hoping somehow somebody will find a cure. Our unspoken fear is that if not, the Situation may prove malignant.

In the heavy time since the Intifada broke out our story has descended from hope to shock to despair to nihilistic acceptance. Even I and my family, who have emerged relatively unscathed, are damaged and forever changed.

Chapter Two

Peace Falters Before Our Eyes

In our section of the world it is impossible to point a finger and say, "Here, here is where the conflict started." Or "Here, here is where the peace started." The struggle for possession and ascendancy has pounded on for over a hundred years, since the first Zionist dreamers arrived in the 1880s to drain the swamps and reestablish a Jewish presence in the Holy Land. The history books are full of misguided epithets, from former Egyptian president Gamal Abdel Nasser's vow to drive Israel into the sea to the Zionist slogan, "A people without a land for a land without a people."

The bloodletting is not new to this decade, or the one before, or the one before that. In 1929 sixty-seven Jews were massacred in Hebron by the town's Arab inhabitants. On the eve of the 1956 Sinai campaign Israeli soldiers mowed down forty-seven Israeli Arabs in violation of curfew in the village of Kfar Kassem. The British who ruled the country from 1919 until 1948 could do little more than walk a tightrope between the aspirations of the Jews and those of the Arabs. From the time the State of Israel was established in 1948, the Arab–Israeli conflict has been its most virulent and persistent characteristic.

The Arabs and Jews have fought four wars outright: the 1948 War of Independence, the 1956 Sinai Campaign, the 1967 Six-Day War, and the 1973 Yom Kippur War. But there never seems to have been one solitary year without bloodshed between the peoples.

Yet for several years in the 1990s it looked like the dark tunnel was coming to an end. World leaders, the leaders of the Palestinian and Israeli peoples, and millions of private citizens fervently believed that the time had come, not that lions would lie down with lambs, but that Israelis and Palestinians had found a way to face each other with pens in hand across tables instead of stalking one another with guns and knives across a countryside pitted with innumerable bullets.

For me the first real taste of peace came in October 1991 as I wound my way up the Israeli coast toward the northern coastal town of Acre. During the two-hour drive I had the radio tuned to live reports of a conference about to start in Madrid.

There had always been rumors of private meetings between Israelis and Arabs. As far back as 1947 and 1948 Golda Meir met secretly with Jordan's King Abdullah, who himself was to be assassinated in 1951 by a Palestinian fearful that Abdullah would make a peace deal with Israel. Moshe Dayan was variously reported to have met Arab leaders in Europe. Ground was broken by the 1979 bilateral peace treaty between Israel and Egypt. But it wasn't until the Madrid conference that an international gathering took place that gave comprehensive Israeli–Palestinian peace an official and open agenda. As I drove up the coast I listened to the fanfare of the opening.

Arriving in Acre, I crossed the run-down Jewish section and parked my car outside the even more run-down Arab part of town. I walked through the teeming market of uneven quality. Hung on dirty strings from door beams of shops the cheapest plastic toys swayed in the wind. I saw deflated soccer balls and little dolls with baby bottles encased in plastic that had hung outdoors so long their molding was thick with grime. Coarse skirts, polyester sweaters, nylon scarves, and Arab galabiehs swayed on wire hangers like overdried laundry.

The smells of falafel and lamb wafted from tiny dark restaurants, in front of which the proprietors called out to me, "Madam, Miss, come in for a tasty treat!" I knew from other meals I had in Acre that it was true. Amidst the junk would appear little stores with striking handmade silver jewelry that could compete in beauty with boutique displays in the capitals of the West. But as soon as I slowed my pace to linger, the shop owner bustled outside, impeaching me to take a look. When I heard the supplication "I have something beautiful for you!" I hastened away, put off by the hard sell that was sure to follow.

And yet Acre was intriguing—authentic, with friendly no-nonsense people going about their lives. It is a town that both Arabs and Jews call home, although they live in separate neighborhoods.

The tiny alleyways ended at the run-down port where by noontime fishermen idled, going through their morning catch and mending nets. I walked atop Acre's seaside ramparts built by the Crusaders, among the thick black cannons still standing from Napoleon's unsuccessful siege of the city in 1799.

I wondered how many of the residents of Acre on that sunny morning knew that in Madrid momentous events were taking place.

It seemed fitting at the dawn of peace to visit this provincial town seemingly out of history's way, but whose very own history included Alexander the Great, Julius Caesar, and Napoleon.

In the afternoon I attended a five-hour-long, award-winning, experimental theater drama performed by a mixed cast of Jewish and Arab actors entitled *Arbeit Macht Frei*—"Work Makes One Free"—the sardonic motto on the gates of Auschwitz. At its start an Arab tour guide accompanied the small audience to nearby Kibbutz Lohamei Haghetaot (Ghetto-Fighters Kibbutz). There he gave us a guided tour of the Holocaust museum, stopping in particular in front of the floor-size model replicating Treblinka, explaining with a pointer in his Arabic accent about the exact intake procedure at the camp that led directly to the gas chambers. Only in the course of the performance did it become clear that our guide was in fact one of the actors. The show explored the themes of memorials, remembrance, and the tortured path that led the vanquished to turn into conquerors. Linked in my mind are *Arbeit Macht Frei*, the Arab section of Acre, and the day when Israelis saw evidence they might begin to pull themselves out of a century-long vise of war.

The Madrid conference was followed by the even more important Oslo conference and accords of 1993. One of the two historical events I ever saved on videotape stands on my shelf, in between old children's tapes of *Pinocchio* and *The Little Mermaid*. The label, on which I wrote in black marker, "Peace ceremony, Israel/PLO [Palestine Liberation Organization], September 13, 1993," has faded to near illegibility. When I and my excited family watched Israeli Prime Minister Yitzhak Rabin, Palestinian leader Yasser Arafat, and U.S. President Bill Clinton shaking hands on the White House lawn, we imagined we might go back to watch it in later years with joy.

Just as I had gone to Egypt the year after the two countries signed a peace treaty, I visited Jordan shortly after the 1994 treaty. Egypt was sui generis, like the Canadian Rockies or the Taj Mahal. But whereas Cairo's teeming multitudes, papyri on the muddy Nile, Herodotus' graffiti on the Colossus of Memni, the underground world at Luxor, and the towering Rameses statues at Abu Simbel opened an astounding world, Jordan was another story altogether.

I expected the exotic, yet what Jordan most reminded me of was where I had just left. The Arabs of Jordan were similar to the Arabs I saw in Israel; the topography was analogous, too. They had beautiful Roman ruins, we had beautiful Roman ruins. They had canyons, we had canyons. They had desert, we had desert. Amman was a new city with little atmosphere, Tel Aviv was a new city with little atmosphere. In the midst of Amman stand the ruins of the ancient city called Philadelphia, in the midst of Tel Aviv stands the 4,000-year-old port of Jaffa. The Jordan River was there too, seemingly on the wrong side. It was with an Alice

in Wonderland feeling that I looked across the Dead Sea to see the Israeli coast across the water. To me, Jordan was a mirror image of Israel.

Then the tour bus stopped at Mount Nebo. I stood on the summit
where the exiled Moses had looked down upon the Promised Land that
God had forbidden him to enter. Through the mist the green and
golden fields of Israel shimmered in the horizon. Just as in the time of
Moses, the Jews and other native peoples were fighting over its possession. But it was a propitious moment to be standing on his spot.
Things were on the point of change.

Suddenly everywhere you looked in Israel the unbelievable seemed
to be happening. There was medical cooperation, Israeli and Arab archaeologists on joint digs, Israeli and Arab artists' exhibitions, tour
groups, a Jordanian spa on the Dead Sea catering to Israelis, a casino
in Jericho frequented daily by thousands of Israelis, investments in
factories, Palestinian students in Israeli colleges, even ornithologists
tracking bird migrations across the borders. Little by little, cars appeared on Israeli highways with the white license plates and green
numbers issued by the newly created Palestinian Authority.

In 1997 I sat in a packed auditorium at a binational writers' conference as passionate speeches were simultaneously translated into
Hebrew, Arabic, and English. In 1999 I joined a women's walk for peace
in which Jewish and Arab women turned out 5,000 strong on the Israel–
Jordan border.

One Saturday I attended a bazaar in the courtyard of a small museum in Tel Aviv on Bialik Street, where early Zionists made their
homes, including the poet after whom the street is now named. Crowded
into the garden were tables of Bedouin jewelry, embroidery, woven
baskets, and plates brimming with Arab cakes. The Palestinian women
from Tulkarem and Nablus shyly selling their handicrafts had never
been to Tel Aviv before, and many of the Israelis circulating among
the booths were only familiar with the Palestinian towns as newspaper
headlines. The bazaar was organized by Touch in Peace, an obscure
binational women's group founded by an Israeli homeopathic phar-

macy in Tel Aviv that initiated a volunteer homeopathic health clinic in Ramallah. The bazaar was one of many modest grassroots happenings amidst the larger plans afoot.

Palestinians from the territories still needed work permits in Israel, but they seemed freely given, and Palestinian laborers were a visible everyday sight working in construction, in hotels, and in restaurants. But their menial status and the often harsh conditions of their employment raised painful questions of how the Israeli state, which once prized socialist ideals, was turning into a de facto champion of capitalism built upon the backs of cheap labor. This less than pristine treatment of the Palestinian work force and the resentments it engendered were the subject of Israeli author David Grossman's exposé *The Yellow Wind*, published in 1988, the same year that the first Intifada exploded.

Despite the grumblings of doom-and-gloomniks and hard-liners, it was a time of heady euphoria. Yet the coming peace never stopped being fiercely debated in Israel. The war of the bumper stickers was one manifestation. People started to wear their ideologies on their automobiles.

"Peace now" was the obvious slogan of the peace camp, sometimes written in Arabic as well as Hebrew. The opposition was more creative: "There is no Zionism without Zion."

The most famous sticker of all, which said simply, "The People is with the Golan," was put up on windows and strung across roadside boulders. It meant Israel should return the Golan Heights it had captured from Syria in 1967.

For the Six-Day War of 1967 had gained Israel enormous territories over and above the West Bank and the Gaza Strip. In the south it conquered the whole Sinai Peninsula, a vast wilderness of mountains, deserts, canyons, and 120 miles of coastline along the Red Sea. Israelis were mesmerized by its beauty and open spaces. One New Year's Eve my husband and I traveled to the 1,400-year-old Greek Orthodox monastery of Saint Catherine on a 5,000-foot-high plateau in the granite mountains, slept in the unheated dormitory rented out to tourists, and rose at 3 a.m. to make the steep nighttime climb up Mount Sinai. We arrived at the summit at sunrise, where legend claims that Moses received the Ten Commandments, and as the light broke we saw a vista of barren mountains in an emptiness reminiscent of the moon.

Most appealing of all was the untouched coastline. Every holiday thousands upon thousands drove south, often with wind surfs tied to their car roofs, to pitch tents along the pristine sea. Merely floating atop the water's surface with a simple snorkel afforded a visual feast of the world's richest collection of tropical fish and coral reefs.

Israel gave up the entire Sinai Peninsula in 1982 as part of its peace accord with Egypt. The northern Sinai settlement of Yamit was bull-dozed by the Israelis prior to its return to Egypt. In the southern Sinai, the farmers who had set up melon farms and small hotels simply pulled up and left. The settlement that they had called Neviot resumed its prior Arab name of Nuweiba. The displaced Israelis received compensation from the Israeli government, but for long afterward many felt unable to emotionally compensate for parting from the best years of their lives spent beside the Red Sea.

After Sinai was returned to Egypt, Israelis didn't stop coming, and neither did my family and I. We left the southernmost Israeli city of Eilat, stood on long lines to have our passports stamped by Israeli border officials, and then again a few yards later by the Egyptians. At first we stayed at hotels Israelis had built, which changed their names and their ownership. Right at the gateway to the Sinai five minutes from the border, the Israeli Avia Sonesta became the Taba Hilton. Over the years entrepreneurs built apartments and hotels all along the coast, erasing the splendid isolation. Just as the once exotic Eilat had fit into the spectacular landscape of granite mountains ending at dark blue sea only to burgeon into an ugly, poor-man's replica of Las Vegas, the Egyptian Sinai too was on its way to becoming commercialized and tacky.

At the other end of the country, the Golan Heights, conquered from Syria in 1967, still remains in Israeli hands three and a half decades later. Kibbutzim and small towns were established, and upon its soil were born the first Israeli wine labels to seriously compete in the international market.

In the Hermon mountain range, 9,200 feet at its highest peak, Israelis opened a populist ski resort, built cable cars, rented ski equipment, and created a ski patrol unit of the army.

In 1981 Israel annexed the Golan Heights, thus incorporating it into the country. Yet in the mid-1990s, when Israelis thought peace was almost a fait accompli, they felt that any settlement would mean that the Golan, or at least large parts of it, would be relinquished. The Golan issue triggered a national schism, hence the bumper stickers. To the sticker "The People is with the Golan," the leftists countered, "Peace is greater than the Greater Israel."

A national mania each winter was born to drive up to enjoy the Hermon "one last time." As soon as temperatures dipped and the snow began to fall, there was a pilgrimage northward to visit once more "before we give it back."

The Golan Heights gave Israel breathing space. To Israelis crammed into a tiny country it seemed as vast as the steppes of Russia, or the endless plains of the midwestern United States. For decades, Israelis had watched the snow-covered Hermon from afar. Suddenly they could drive up a road and see the clouds below them.

In the spring they trekked through wild flowers up to their waists, marveled at the raptors circling overhead, and climbed the ruins of Gamla, an ancient city documented by the Roman historian Josephus Flavius.

They built field schools and discovered ancient synagogues. They excavated Roman baths, bottled spring water, opened a crocodile zoo, and frolicked in hot mineral pools.

On a Saturday in January, Mount Hermon became as crowded as the beach in Tel Aviv at high noon in July. The radio broadcast traffic advisories of rush-hour congestion on the two-lane roads. Families unused to cold arrived in droves, wearing layers of sweaters and shoes not meant for snow. People with no business on skis careened across the slopes, middle-aged men cavorted like kindergartners, lines for the cable car recalled Disneyland, parking lots were jammed, and children zigzagged down hills on sleds fashioned out of grocery cartons. Come midweek the mountain was empty again, dotted only by hikers or skiers who rose at 5 a.m. in Tel Aviv or Jerusalem to be on the trails by 9.

To the 18,000 Jewish and 17,000 Druze Moslems who call the Golan home, its majesty inspired a fierce love. The Jewish residents felt that if they would have to leave, the frontier would follow in their hearts. To the strategists the Golan represented a territorial security buffer. To millions of Israelis it was a taste of infinity. The Golan was Israel's Big Sky country, its nights offering carpets of stars elsewhere dimmed by the electricity of civilization.

Whenever my husband returns to the Golan, he recalls the star-studded sky he saw when he was sent there as an army doctor during the 1973 October war, when Syria attacked. Soldiers camped in makeshift tents or dispersed in sleeping bags under the sky in expectation of commando raids. During that war young soldiers were killed in exploding tanks, and helicopters dodged the shells to land beside field hospitals and evacuate the wounded. Despite its peaceful appearance, Golan soil is riddled with the old land mines of both sides, rusty but still lethal.

Having had a taste of trekking through virgin snow and watching the eagles soar, Israelis internalized its magic. Even those most willing to give it up found it a bitter separation.

But the years dragged by, and no final peace talks ever materialized. The Golan is still very much part of Israel. Yet in the mid-1990s separation seemed imminent.

If one man personified the new era, it was Yitzhak Rabin, who took over from the hard-line right winger Yitzhak Shamir to become prime minister in 1992. Results of the shift of ideology were immediately felt in a most prosaic way. Highways in the country had long been neglected, and the surge in the number of passenger cars had spawned traffic jams from hell. But the Shamir government had relentlessly poured its resources into building roads throughout the West Bank for the expanding Jewish settlements while neglecting the country's infrastructure. As soon as Rabin won, bulldozers appeared overnight to begin widening the high-ways within the Green Line. That Green Line, which really is drawn in green on my road maps, marks the borders between the country as it was constituted in 1949 and the West Bank it captured in 1967.

It is often said that Israeli society is a small one. It will rarely hap-pen that an Israeli music lover going to the Israel Philharmonic will not bump into at least one acquaintance at every concert. The same is true of a football fan attending a game. But as a newcomer, I often felt it to be insular and self-contained. As I live here longer, I too have begun to recognize familiar faces in the crowd.

Still I don't have the network of people who grew up here—a friend in the police, a friend in the university administration, a friend in the building committee of the municipality, a friend on the management of El Al. Israel, for all its Western pretensions, remains a society where connections are arguably better than money. In Hebrew slang it is "protectzia"—knowing the right person in the right place.

Even after decades here, I have almost negligible protectzia. But my husband's position as a leading physician puts him in contact with many key individuals. Through him, I had the opportunity to personally meet, second only to David Ben-Gurion, the most famous Israeli of all.

I had actually seen Yitzhak Rabin on dozens of Saturday mornings when, as minister of defense, he came to engage in his lifelong hobby, coincidentally the same as mine: tennis. As I played my Saturday morn-ing doubles game in the Dan Accadia Tennis Club in Herzliya, it was always clear when Rabin was expected. His arrival with his wife, Leah, was preceded by a contingent of two or three plainclothes security men. They went from court to court checking the periphery with sensors, looking through the shrubbery, and even casting perfunctory glances into our tennis bags strewn upon the benches. A little later, a white car pulled into the parking lot, and then Rabin and his wife walked down the path. One security guard accompanied them onto the court. The guards wore their unmistakable ubiquitous garb of beige pants, navy shirt, and dark sunglasses; the rest of the guards drank coffee on the veranda, little telephone wires sticking out of their shirts and fitting into one ear. We used to smile at the whole procedure. It was hard to take seriously the need for such protection at our peaceful courts beside the Mediterranean.

After Rabin became prime minister he stopped coming to the Accadia on Saturday morning. Even though he was not an observant Jew, it would be considered needlessly provocative of prevalent religious sensibilities for a prime minister to be seen driving on the Sabbath. From then on he and his wife played at the courts near their home in Ramat Aviv, a suburb closer to Tel Aviv.

It was to the Rabins' apartment in Ramat Aviv that I joined my husband as a dinner guest in the autumn of 1994. There was no sign in the lobby that it was the home of the country's prime minister. As the elevator doors opened onto their floor there was a lone guard at a table outside the Rabin apartment who checked our names and consulted a list before buzzing us in.

The occasion was a dinner for an eminent doctor from Boston. He arrived accompanied by his wife. She stood in the background during cocktails, and when asked she described herself as "just a housewife from New England." The party was a small one, perhaps a dozen invitees, including other doctors and high-powered lawyers. It was an assortment of the articulate, the powerful, and the outspoken.

The meal was served around the dining table, which stood in one corner of the living room. Rabin sat at one end and his wife at the other. The doctor from Boston was seated next to Leah Rabin, and the doctor's wife, apparently as per protocol, found her place at the prime minister's right. The conversation glittered with political insights and clever stories. But Rabin's behavior floored me; the prime minister's attention was focused throughout on his unglamorous companion. He told her anecdotes and whispered translations when someone at the table lapsed into Hebrew. Rabin had the reputation for being a shy and reticent man, somewhat socially maladroit. Yet what I saw that one time I met him was something else: simple kindness toward the very guest whom nobody else would have paid any attention to.

The next time I saw Rabin I was standing in a crowd among tens of thousands of others. From a podium in Tel Aviv, Rabin addressed a rally to celebrate the course he had so unequivocally espoused. It was Saturday night, November 4, 1995.

Beside Rabin were Foreign Minister Shimon Peres and other dignitaries, artists, and personalities. Another man who stood in a place of honor was an eclectic flamboyant character, an individual who single-handedly began the Israeli peace movement years before Rabin or any other sober-minded Israeli dared to step out on that limb. Abie Nathan, dismissed as an eccentric crackpot, a man who never held any public office, was the guru of the Israeli peace movement. In fact, he was its minister without portfolio.

Born in Iran and brought up in India, Abie Nathan arrived in Israel in 1948 to volunteer for Israel's infant air force. During the War of Independence he flew arms from Czechoslovakia. He remained in the air force until 1951, when like many military pilots, he moved over to commercial flying; for approximately the next decade he was a pilot for El Al airlines. Nathan then opened a gourmet restaurant in Tel Aviv, became part of the city's bohemia, and drank and partied hard. His financial success allowed him to turn for the rest of his life to fulfilling a vision of philanthropy and peace. He credited his devotion in part to expunging the guilt he carried for once having been a fighter pilot.

In 1966, when Israeli and Arab children imagined each other as having horns, Abie Nathan took off in a single-engine plane for an unauthorized flight across the Sinai Desert into Egypt. When his "peace plane" landed in Egypt the exasperated Egyptians sent the crackpot right back across the border. The Israelis didn't know how to handle Nathan any better than the enemy did.

In the summer of 1965, when I visited Israel as a teenager, I sat in Nathan's unlikely peace headquarters, housed in his trendy Tel Aviv hamburger bar that Nathan called California. Peace notices were chalked on a folding blackboard announcing the countdown to his upcoming flight to Egypt, but it seemed Nathan was the only activist, and few took him seriously.

Nathan continued his crusade, embarking upon a new venture that would become a regional institution. He bought an old ship, anchored it just outside Israel's territorial waters, and in 1973 began the radio station he called the "Voice of Peace." The off-shore Voice of Peace was a pirate station, a commercial enterprise with a mission. Nathan became the Robin Hood of the airwaves, and he relished the role.

Day in and day out, the Voice of Peace offered rock music interspersed with ideals. Its slogan was repeated in English, Hebrew, and Arabic. It announced that it was anchored "somewhere in the Mediterranean." In reality, the Peace Ship was just off the Israeli coast and could be seen by bathers on the public beach. But if Nathan stretched the truth a few nautical miles, it was in the name of romanticism, and people forgave him for it. For in a line of pioneers who had come to Israel with a dream, Nathan was the last, and perhaps the greatest, Israeli romantic.

The Voice of Peace broadcast a plea for "peace, love, and human understanding" from Tyre to Tivon, from Alexandria to Ashkelon. Every evening as the sun set, Nathan read a passage from Kahlil Gibran's *The Prophet*. Then the station suspended its transmission for a minute of silence in memory of "the victims of violence in our area and around the world at large."

Nathan supported a variety of causes promoting Arab–Israeli coexistence. He donated to the pediatric wing of the Sheba Medical Center because it treated Palestinian children, equipping it with the first pediatric cardiac monitors in the Middle East.

His humanitarianism extended further. In 1968, when he learned of the mounting death toll among Biafrans caught in the Nigerian civil war, Nathan himself went to Biafra, bringing food he had purchased. Throughout the years he organized aid for victims of earthquakes and volcanoes worldwide, always making the biggest donations himself.

For decades, Nathan was Israel's self-appointed goodwill ambassador. Of course, no Israeli government would officially send him anywhere—he was too politically hot. Nathan was always marginal, a fringe personality, a beloved symbol of somebody who marched to his own drummer.

In the late 1980s Nathan traveled abroad to speak with representatives of the Palestine Liberation Organization when doing so was still a criminal offense. He was brought to trial, sentenced to 18 months in prison, and incarcerated for several months.

One Saturday I happened to drive past Nathan's prison, and saw dozens of supporters who had come to visit and cheer him up. They gathered outside the barbed-wire gates, waving and singing—young men carrying toddlers on their shoulders and young women holding up handwritten signs of solidarity.

The first time I laid eyes on him in 1978, the normally portly Nathan was emaciated from over 50 days of a hunger strike and close to collapse. I and my 5-year-old daughter had come with Dalia and Dan, our first Israel next-door neighbors who became dear friends, to my first peace demonstration in Tel Aviv. Amidst the flickering of 10,000 candles, Nathan painfully rose to the podium. A mere shadow in a white suit, he urged the Israeli government to "give peace a chance."

Seventeen years later, my now grown-up daughter and I watched him in the same spot, singing peace songs beside Yitzhak Rabin. Nathan was beaming. His lonely cause had finally become mainstream.

The demonstration that night had an aura of celebration, not the sense of struggle we were used to from peace rallies in Israel. As the crowd sang and swayed, strangers with their arms around each other singing the "Song of Peace," I recognized the same magnetism that electrified the antiwar Vietnam rallies in the United States in the 1960s.

Before my daughter and I went out that evening, my husband had warned me to be careful, to keep my distance. "Look around you," he cautioned. "They are expecting violence." The right wing had been excoriating Rabin and the peace movement in scathing terms. I hurried out, though, worrying about where I would find parking. After the singing ended, I linked my arm through my daughter's and asked smugly, "Do you think it's peaceful enough here tonight for Daddy?"

The rally dispersed and I returned to my car, passing by policemen and soldiers with arms dangling by their sides, watching the crowd file out.

Minutes later as I drove home, I saw squads of police cars, sirens flashing, suddenly appear from nowhere. I turned on the radio, and heard the unbelievable news.

Three bullets had aborted it all.

Rabin had been shot by a single assailant. Yigal Amir was a young law student, a religious Jew, and a political fanatic. Even as the police surrounded the assassin, bodyguards stuffed Rabin's bullet-ridden body into the back of his private car. His terrified chauffeur sped the mortally wounded man toward the nearest hospital.

"I called back over my shoulder to ask him how he felt," sobbed the driver in a radio interview the following day. And from where he lay slumped an hour short of death, Rabin reassured the driver.

"It hurts," Rabin told him. "But it's not terrible. No, not terrible." Later the bloodstained paper bearing the lyrics of the "Song of Peace" were found in Rabin's breast pocket.

Yitzhak Rabin was the antithesis of the swaggering, bragging, over-confident, shoot-from-the-hip personality one has come to expect from a career general chosen to be prime minister of a feisty country with a chip on its shoulder. The tragedy of the nation lay almost as much in the loss of Rabin's persona as in the loss of his policies. And perhaps the two were not so different. The individual who made a habit of putting the shy, the nonpowerful, and the working person first became for a short time the head of state who put humanity before land and life before grandeur.

After Rabin was shot, and before his death was announced, Abie Nathan was interviewed on TV. His words were muffled and incoherent.

He wept unabashedly. Nathan had attended all the peace rallies. It looked like November 4, 1995, might be his last.

The other videotape that sits on my shelf is the footage of Yitzhak Rabin's funeral. I turned it on for a short time not long ago, but almost a decade later it is too painful to watch for long. I again saw U.S. presidents Bill Clinton, Jimmy Carter, and George Bush (the elder), England's Prince Charles, French President Jacques Chirac, German Chancellor Helmut Kohl, and Egyptian President Hosni Mubarak among the world's top dignitaries assembled before the coffin on Mount Herzl. And most touching of all, there was Rabin's partner in peace, Jordan's King Hussein, the man who had sneaked a smoke together with Rabin in the White House, the man who had become his friend. Hussein was to die of cancer four years later. But in 1995 he looked strong and vibrant, and delivered his eloquent eulogy in resonant English. "I never thought a moment would come when I would grieve the loss of a friend and colleague . . . who met us on the opposite side of a divide." Hussein took his leave of Rabin: "You lived as a soldier; you died as a soldier for peace."

A few days later in her apartment in Ramat Aviv, the apartment where I had gone to the Rabins' dinner party, Leah Rabin received a condolence visit from Yasser Arafat.

The square where Rabin had last stood was renamed after him. It glowed for weeks with the sad light of memorial candles.

Peace stickers became passé. All over Israel two new stickers appeared. "Shalom, Haver"—"Goodbye, friend"—one said, the words Clinton had used to end his eulogy to Rabin. The other sticker was a black bordered white rectangle, mimicking a death notice, and on it solely numbers, the date that brought the short peace era to an abrupt close: "4.11.95."

If it was impossible to pinpoint when the conflict started, or the process that tried to resolve it, the night of November 4, 1995 triggered hope's demise. Of all the dates in Israel's cataclysmic history, this was the blackest.

Shimon Peres inherited the sad reins of government. But he could not carry on the peace momentum. Radical Palestinian elements resumed suicide bombings with a vengeance. The following May, Peres badly lost the election for prime minister to right-wing Benjamin ("Bibi") Netanyahu. Just as the country hadn't seen Rabin's death coming, neither did the peace camp predict the Peres debacle. It was said that complaisance helped in his defeat, as well as a disastrous television debate, in which Peres gamely tried to keep his own against the charisma of spin-master Netanyahu.

Peres, the grand old statesman of Israel, now in his 80s, whose eloquence still makes listeners gasp, has what they used to call "Jewish eyes." Their sadness gives them away. Even when he smiles his gaze never quite shakes off the hint of tragedy. And as the ancient Greeks observed, character is destiny. That premonition of loss leaps out from Peres's eyes.

But before the 1996 election, I and the people around me did not see what was coming. Living in the cocoon of my own conviction, I hardly knew one acquaintance who supported Netanyahu, and thought it inconceivable that he would win.

Only when I drove through the countryside two days before the election and passed hills plastered with giant banners predicting an upset did the unthinkable take shape and form.

On election day, while officials of Peres's Labor Party went docilely to observe formalities at polling booths, officials of Netanyahu's Likud Party drove indefatigably through the streets of Jerusalem, back and forth for hours on end, their loudspeakers turned up full volume, urging every last eligible body to get out and cast a ballot.

More than anything else, Netanyahu turned on his charisma and his charm, turning the medium into the message. Their televised debate was reminiscent of Kennedy outshining Nixon on TV during the first "image" campaign of 1960. Peres wore makeup resembling the victim of a small-town embalmer, whereas "Bibi" conveyed the vigor of a movie star.

In the annus horribilis of 1995–96 we lost Rabin—and then we let Peres slip through our fingers. We gaped at Rabin's murder, and felt guilty that we hadn't seen that character assassination can lead to physical annihilation. Then when Peres lost it was only a matter of time before the peace he and Rabin spearheaded together would fall victim too.

Yet in May 1999 the pendulum swung left once again, when Netanyahu was soundly trounced at the polls by Israel's Labor Party candidate Ehud Barak. Although Barak was a military man turned politician, his administration was widely viewed in Israel as a reaffirmation of Israel's commitment to the peace process. I went to friends in Tel Aviv to listen to the results of what we viewed as a momentous election night. As Netanyahu made his concession speech only a few minutes after the polls closed, a giant roar could be heard through the windows of the apartment open to the spring night. It was the crowd filling the same square where Rabin had been assassinated, now cheering at what they saw as the resurrection of Rabin's course.

But the cheers were premature. While those around me in Israel assumed that Israel was implementing the Oslo agreements and subsequent Wye accords, to the Palestinians, Israeli compliance appeared lagging.

The peace process began to stagnate. Bellicose voices within both societies gained confidence. When the second Intifada began in September 2000, both sides accused the other for its instigation. "Barak offered everything to Arafat on a silver platter," said Israelis, referring to the failed Camp David meetings two months before the Intifada. "What Israel offered were nothing but Bantustans," responded the Palestinians. Recrimination became the order of the day.

Peace had almost crossed the threshold. Then it retreated.

After Rabin's death, Abie Nathan left the country. The man who had been a symbol for a generation seemed to have run out of steam. Shortly before his 70th birthday a few years later, Nathan suffered a stroke. Returning home in a wheelchair he mumbled to reporters in slurred speech, "On my tombstone let it be written: 'Abie Nathan—I tried.'"

Chapter Three

Jerusalem: A State of Mind

Only 40 miles of up-to-date highway separate Jerusalem and Tel Aviv, but each city is a different Israel. Where Jerusalem recently celebrated its 3,000th birthday, Tel Aviv has been around for only nine decades. Where Jerusalem is sedate, Tel Aviv is brash. Where Jerusalem is cultured, Tel Aviv is vulgar. Jerusalem is cool and dry, Tel Aviv is hot and humid. Jerusalem is Levantine, Tel Aviv is European. Jerusalem closes down early at night, Tel Aviv bills itself as "the city without interruption." Jerusalem is the seat of government, Tel Aviv is the heart of commerce. Jerusalem is in the mountains, Tel Aviv is by the sea. Jerusalem is stately, Tel Aviv is pedestrian. Jerusalem is exotic, Tel Aviv is monochrome. Jerusalem is religious, Tel Aviv is secular. In my eyes, Jerusalem is beautiful, and Tel Aviv is ugly.

I love Jerusalem. But I live near Tel Aviv.

I've always felt that had Jerusalem been my home, I would have been a better me. I would have kept the important things in mind. I would have resolved the unresolved questions, or at least made a serious stab at it. I would feel a part of history, instead of an occasional visitor.

Pinned on the wall of my study is a fading photocopied sheet announcing an evening lecture on Freud and Kafka given several years ago at an institute in Jerusalem. I keep it there as a reminder of what I thought was awaiting me when I moved to Israel. I imagined a round of open-to-the-public lectures tucked away in Spartan meeting halls, packed with intense, eccentric, but friendly people—lectures on the Enlightenment and the kabala, on Maimonides and Einstein, on writers Shalom Aleichem and Y. L. Peretz, on composer Felix Mendelssohn and artist Amedeo Modigliani, on philosophers Hannah Arendt and Baruch Spinoza. Upon the centenary of the death of Zionist visionary Theodor Herzl in 2004 I heard of an intriguing three-day conference, "Herzl: Then and Now." In Jerusalem—where else?

Instead, I have lived all my Israeli life on the coast near aggressive, pragmatic Tel Aviv. In my world, it's been more traffic updates than lectures. And despite the magnificence of the alternately turquoise and wine-dark sea, the vistas of oranges heavy in green orchards, and the fields of sunflowers turning their faces in unison toward the sun, I never felt at the country's core.

It changes nothing that I see the weekend papers list a myriad of similarly soul-enriching events in Tel Aviv. Even if I attend, I know they would feel more significant in Jerusalem.

There I would emerge into the limpid night, tread on narrow sidewalks beside old stone walls, on curving streets bearing the names of kings and queens who had made that same Jerusalem their home. I would see the ramparts of the Old City lit up, glimpse the Tower of David shining in the distance.

They say Tel Aviv is cosmopolitan, throbbing, vibrant, the cutting edge. In Jerusalem events arrive and change more slowly. Maybe it is for the better. If Tel Aviv is cosmopolitan, it is also strident.

In adolescent Tel Aviv when people speak of history they mean the British Mandate. Jerusalem predates London and Paris and Rome. It had already lived through a golden age when Athens was but a work in progress. No matter how many modern buildings go up, in Jerusalem millennia dog its steps.

When Manhattan was still a forested wilderness, miniature Jerusalem skylines were cast on silver wedding plates in medieval Mainz. Almost every ancient cartographer drew Jerusalem at his map's heart. For 2,000 years not a single day has passed without its name being called out loud or mouthed in prayer—in the Medici's Florence, in Franz Joseph's Vienna, in Peron's Argentina, in Franklin Roosevelt's Washington, in Catherine's St. Petersburg. "Jerusalem" existed within them all.

The city is majestic in its timelessness, yet wears that majesty enigmatically. And when I visit, weaving between its many faces, I too imbibe a little of each identity: the exoticism of oriental bazaars, the inspiration of spires and domes and arches, the stateliness of national buildings, the sorrow of memorials.

Jerusalem is extreme. There is no heat spell hotter than in Jerusalem, no cold more piercing, no wind more bitter, no rain more torrential. But in contrast there is no sky bluer, no rose as fragrant, no spring sweeter. Cypress trees grow all over the country, but in Jerusalem they soar.

Jerusalem is more than a city, more than the sum of its buildings. It is a metropolis inseparable from an idea. At the height of the marriage ceremony the Jewish groom repeats the Psalmist pledge, "If I forget thee, O Jerusalem, let my right hand forget her cunning. If I do not remember thee, let my tongue cleave to the roof of my mouth: if I prefer not Jerusalem above my chief joy." Even the most secular of Jews knows the sentence that rings out at every Passover seder around the globe: "Next year in Jerusalem." Every Jew is a Jerusalemite, even if he never sets foot there.

While in most Israeli towns the municipality erects a metal sign to welcome incoming motorists, the driver, rounding the curve into this city's outskirts, meets an enormous botanical tablet that meticulously spells out "Blessed be your arrival in Jerusalem." As I end the long climb

from the seacoast to arrive at the pinnacle of the country, this green
welcome ushers me in to a city it takes a lifetime to explore.

I've built the fantasy that life would have been more fulfilling by
choosing to rise to Jerusalem's cool mornings and bed down beneath
its clear stars.

Yet in fairness, I realize not. Perhaps if I made it my home, the
prosaic would have predominated as in every other place: the race not
to miss the bus, to get the children to school on time, the frustrations
of standing on lines, of making the bank before it closed, of dentist
appointments and shoe repair. In short, of juggling the mundane, of
striving to get through the day with one's equilibrium intact.

So maybe it is better I still have Jerusalem as a jewel wrapped in its
box of mystery, to keep as a special destination where I never can enter
without excitement, or ever leave without regret. Jerusalem exists not
only at latitude 31°47'N and longitude 35°13'E. For me, Jerusalem is
a state of mind.

But Jerusalem is not just a Jewish city, not in ideology and not in
population. From the Stations of the Cross on the Via Dolorosa to the
room of the Last Supper, Jerusalem is the city of Jesus. Monks, priests,
friars, nuns, ministers of all faiths and in all dress stream through its
streets. Churches abound, from the magnificent to the tiny; among
them are Anglican, Baptist, Lutheran, Seventh Day Adventist, Pres-
byterian, Pentecostal, Catholic, and Franciscan, as well as Armenian,
Coptic, Ethiopian, Romanian, Syrian, Greek, and Russian Orthodox.
My eyes always search the hillside to sight the mushroom spires of the
Russian Orthodox Church. I've stopped by the gift shop of the Scottish church. I've slept in a Polish convent in the Old City. I've listened
to Bach organ recitals in the Benedictine Abbey of the Dormition
within the walls of the Old City.

To Islam only Mecca and Medina surpass Jerusalem in holiness. The
silver-domed Al-Aksa mosque originally built in the eighth century,
restored by the Moslem hero Saladin, and reconstructed during the
British Mandate holds 5,000 worshipers for Friday prayers. The Mosque

of Omar stands nearby, its golden dome brilliant in the sun. Its interior, made of mosaic and gold and encircled by stained-glass windows, is even more beautiful. In days gone by I visited the mosque without apprehension or fear, shedding my shoes at the entrance and treading upon the gorgeous red carpets.

Also known as the Dome of the Rock, the mosque stands upon the spot where Mohammed is believed to have made his mystic flight to heaven. In Judaism it is the site of the altar upon which Abraham was commanded to sacrifice his son Isaac. It is also the core of the ancient Temple of Solomon, the holiest site in Judaism. At its periphery stands the Western Wall, what remains of that ancient temple.

After the 1948 War of Independence the city was split in two: the Arab sector was in Jordan and the Jewish sector became the capital of Israel. With the Israeli victory in 1967 it came under total Israeli sovereignty. The Israelis say it was "reunited." But its political future has been one of the fundamental stumbling blocks of all peace discussions. Will it be divided once again to become the capital of Israel as well as the capital of Palestine? Will it become an international city? The problem of Jerusalem was viewed as so difficult that, during peace negotiations, decisions regarding its future were always put off until "easier" problems were solved.

In fact, the current Intifada roared to a start after the exhibitionist visit of Ariel Sharon, then minister of defense, to the Temple Mount flanked by a vanguard of security. Sharon, with his long and cloudy military past, was the Israeli whose presence most symbolizes belligerency. If Jerusalem as a whole is problematic, the Temple Mount is the nucleus of disputed sovereignty. Usually the Israeli government walks a careful line particularly regarding this location, trying to permit access to both faiths, and doing its best to avoid controversy. But it is often from there that violence between Arabs and Jews erupts. Maybe Sharon's high-profile visit was not the underlying cause of the Intifada, but it provided an ostentatious trigger. Nothing could have been more provocative. To differentiate it from the "first" Intifada in the late 1980s to early 1990s, the current Palestinian uprising was dubbed the Al-Aksa Intifada in dubious honor of Sharon's visit.

How many people live in Jerusalem? It depends on whom you ask. The official Israel census listed 630,000 in 1996, 70 percent of them Jews. According to Israeli statistics there are 180,000 non-Jewish residents, the overwhelming majority of them Arab. But the Palestinian census of 1997 reported the Palestinian population as nearly double: 328,601.

Several Arab villages at the periphery have an unclear status. And even if the municipality includes some villages, it may not provide municipal services. The residents are, however, obliged to pay municipal taxes, an obligation, Israelis claim, about which Arab citizens in general are severely remiss. However, in Jerusalem Palestinians may be prodded to pay the bills, because whenever they approach a government ministry the first thing they are asked to produce is their tax receipt.

Who can build, and where, is an explosive issue. Whereas the hills around the city are blanketed with new Jewish neighborhoods built since 1967, Palestinians charge they are paralyzed by the denial of building permits. When they go ahead and construct anyway, their "illegal" dwellings are often demolished by the authorities.

Israel issues residency identity cards to Palestinians for whom Jerusalem is the "major focus" of their life. There is constantly tension by Palestinians trying to obtain this coveted residency status. The reason is mainly economic. Israeli ID cards entitle them to Israeli social services, most notably national health benefits.

This silent side effect of the Israeli–Palestinian struggle over Jerusalem spawns behind-the-scenes dramas that jeopardize everyday life.

One example is Yasser Abu Halaf, a Palestinian teenager who developed malignant brain cancer at age 16. The ninth out of thirteen children, Yasser left school after the sixth grade. Since age 14 he worked as a dishwasher and odd-job boy in a Jerusalem restaurant.

Yasser hid the bump growing on his head as long as he could. After metastatic cancer was diagnosed, he received treatment in a Palestinian hospital, but its facilities were limited. Israelis argue that rich Arab neighbors could well afford to donate to Palestinian health care: "Why can't Saudi Arabia set up a hospital for them—or even donate one CAT scan?" Palestinians counter that if Israel is occupying their territory they should commit to the health needs of its inhabitants. Since the Palestinian Authority (PA) took jurisdiction over infrastructure, the level of services has not improved.

Soon Yasser's family took him to Jerusalem's Hadassah University Medical Center, where he began receiving intensive treatment.

Yasser was born in Jerusalem; so were his parents. They all held Israeli IDs. In the 1980s, unable to afford housing inside the city, the family moved outside the city limits to the village of Kalandia a few miles away.

Kalandia is in what is known as the "seam" between Israeli Jerusalem and the PA, a legal no-man's land where Israel and the PA attempt to throw responsibility for social services upon the other.

The bureaucracy's computers did not pick up Yasser's case for several months, but when they did, the spigot immediately went dry. Arriving one day at the hospital for a chemotherapy treatment, the family was informed that their Israeli residency had been suspended, and with it their health insurance.

Hadassah hospital insisted on halting the expensive treatments unless assured of financial reimbursement.

Not only nature had conspired to give this unlucky boy the worst hand a person can be dealt. The PA refused to provide health benefits to Palestinians from whom Israel has revoked residency. Yasser found himself in limbo, the unwitting casualty of a political struggle about autonomy, borders, statehood, and nationalism.

His modest family was forced to fight not only cancer but the powers-that-be.

But against the odds, Yasser's scenario played out in his favor.

When treatment was halted, the family turned to the Israeli organization Physicians for Human Rights and to a civil rights law association,

Hamoked Center for the Defense of the Individual, which urgently contacted every relevant government agency. Each passed the jurisdictional buck onward like a hot potato.

It seemed like a dead end until Israeli activist journalist Gideon Levy published an exposé of Yasser's case in the newspaper *Haaretz*.

Yasser's problem became a cause célèbre. The father of an Israeli soldier who died in Lebanon was so appalled at the story Levy told that he and other individuals donated thousands of shekels toward the boy's treatment. Israeli national television featured it on prime-time news.

The week following Levy's article the hospital announced that it would continue to provide Yasser treatment without demanding prior coverage commitment. In the ensuing two years, Yasser received treatment—and bills which Hadassah did not insist he pay. Yet his medical care was furnished on ad hoc humanitarian grounds, not formal ones. Hadassah, whose multinational staff treats all people on a nonsectarian basis, was left hanging to bear the bad press and to pick up the tab, which the PA and the Israeli governments refused to touch.

Yasser was not a boy of many words. At the height of ravaging chemotherapy, he answered simply when asked how he was doing. "OK, OK," he nodded at the TV cameras, which broadcast his story all over Israel, managing a brief smile on his puffy face. On his head he wore the familiar backward baseball cap favored by cancer children who have lost their hair.

After protracted battles with legal authorities, Eliahu Abram, the lawyer at Hamoked, finally won. Yasser's residency and health coverage were restored. Perhaps authorities were shamed into lifting Yasser's writ of execution.

Another Palestinian boy—a healthy one—had quite a different experience with Hadassah hospital. During the contentious negotiations over the future of Hebron during the mid-1990s, an Israeli news crew happened upon a group of preadolescent boys playing in a Hebron street. Among them was Immad El-Batch.

Immad and his friends led the news people to the stairwell of his building, past his family's tiny apartment and up to the roof to show them their "secret" lookout on the Israeli soldiers.

Flattered into openness by the sight of TV cameras and microphones, the boys eagerly answered the questions of the TV team. What did they want to be when they grew up? One answered that he wanted to get married and have enough work to support a family. Then Immad responded, speaking in halting Hebrew but with a sure tone. "Everybody in my family is dumb," he said. "None of them could finish school. When I grow up, I want to be a doctor—a doctor to study eyes."

Bright, serious, outspoken, and gregarious, Immad was the personification of the actor in a walk-on part who steals the show. When he spoke of his dream with such vulnerable candor and such optimism, he won over the veteran crew. They knew that the chances of a boy from the family of uneducated Palestinian laborers to become an eye specialist are infinitesimal.

The TV crew members were not the only people whose heart Immad captured. Professor Saul Merin, chief of the ophthalmology unit at the Mount Scopus branch of Hadassah University Medical Center, had watched Immad's words on television. They prompted Merin to invite the boy to his department. Immad's visit was pictured in the press. He stood in his rough woolen sweater, both hands on the dials of an optical machine. With the same calm, serious look with which he had greeted the Israeli crew in the alleys of Hebron, he focused his gaze into the machine. And beside Immad stood a man with gray hair and a white coat, looking over toward the boy like a guardian angel.

Was it positive symbolism that this Palestinian boy was invited by Hadassah, an institution that bears the quote from Jeremiah: "The healing of my people"? And symbolic, too, that this very hospital, which now treats the adjacent Arab and Jewish population, was severed from Israeli access for nineteen years by the 1948 War of Independence? Would the two peoples' sickness be healed by the time he grows up? Would he indeed one day become Dr. Immad El-Batch?

East Jerusalem bears the great concentration of Palestinians, but there is no boundary or sign marking where the East begins. Some Israeli public buildings are also in East Jerusalem, such as the Israeli Ministry of Justice and the District Court, so that black-clad lawyers on their way to a hearing sometimes stop to buy delicious sesame rolls off the wooden carts of Arab street vendors. A knowing purchaser will also request a mélange of powdered spices in which to dip each bite. The vendor pours out the spice into a square of torn-off old newspaper that he twists into a makeshift dispenser. The lawyers finish the bread on the street, wipe the crumbs off their mouths, and continue on their way to court.

Jerusalem's streets still remain mixed, and 99 percent peaceful. In Liberty Park, named after its reproduction of Philadelphia's Liberty Bell, Arab families routinely mingle with Jewish ones. Hospitals are staffed by Arab and Jewish doctors and nurses. The Jewish hotels employ Arab staff. On the two campuses of the Hebrew University, Arab students stroll in groups, speaking Arabic; many young women wear head scarves and long robes. It is very rare, though, to see Arab and Jewish students mingling or sitting together in the cafeteria. Keeping a wary distance, they have little to say to each other.

But in the frequent spells of hostility, Arab areas are unfriendly locales for Jewish visitors. Not only is there an air of anger and resentment, physical attacks also occur. In the winter of 2002, for example, a 25-year-old woman walking on the spacious Sherover promenade between the Jewish neighborhood of Talpiot and the Palestinian village of Jabel Mukaber was stabbed to death in broad daylight by a gang of young Arab boys from the nearby neighborhood of Abu Tor.

The recently built promenade offering spectacular views of Jerusalem's nature quickly became a favorite photo stop for tourist buses as well as a place the locals came to drink coffee and take walks.

One spring evening as part of the offerings of the annual Jerusalem Festival of Arts, my daughter and I sat in a makeshift theater for a whimsical production of music and food called "Mozart in Chocolate" held beside the promenade. Nobody would dream of playing Mozart there now, and if they did, I would never dream of going.

As for tourist buses, they are few and far between. My tour-guide friend Judy's specialty used to be her sought-after seven-hour 'walk through history'; another guide devised a tour of poetic sites for loving couples. They, like most of the colleagues in their profession, have had hardly any work in years.

In modern times, universities have gained the sacrosanct status traditionally accorded to places of worship. It was assumed that a university was ex territoria for terror. But in the summer of 2002 the Mount Scopus campus of the Hebrew University lost that immunity: seven people were killed in the Frank Sinatra cafeteria by a Palestinian maintenance worker. Ever since, wrote Daniel Ben Simon in *Haaretz*, "the university has turned into a fortress. It is fenced in on all sides, and access to the campus is reserved for lecturers, students, workers, and those with special permits . . . The face of the Mount Scopus campus in the past year is the face of Jerusalem."

Over time I have learned to drive to a few locations in Jerusalem, but I am never sure when I start out if I indeed will reach my destination without getting lost, circling, poring over maps, and asking person after person for directions. I have succeeded in mastering the twists and turns of Tel Aviv, but driving into the hodgepodge of Jerusalem is as daunting as facing the illogic of Boston's one-way streets after the comforting geometric symmetry of Manhattan.

In the door pocket of my car I have one road atlas of Israel, one map of the streets of Tel Aviv, one map of the Galilee, and at last count no fewer than five of Jerusalem. I am always apprehensive of taking the wrong road, and winding up where I might be perceived as an unwelcome intruder.

One day my apprehensions were borne out in a way I couldn't have predicted. All my life I have seen myself as a civil libertarian, a liberal, a peacenik. In sum, a democrat. But my behavior proved me to be no better than the most hypocritical old salon communist.

I had driven to the capital to attend an evening meeting, but was delayed in traffic. Night had fallen and I was late. A double outsider, I was frightened of crossing the invisible borders of the "unified" city into territory where, with my poor mastery of direction, I felt I might be an easy target.

I suddenly recalled advice given to me by a fellow American also based in Tel Aviv: When in doubt in Jerusalem, leave your car in the guest parking lot at the former Hilton Hotel at the city's periphery, and hop into a cab.

With relief, that's what I did. Opening the back door I slid into the first cab on the line waiting to collect passengers at the hotel entrance. I was just sitting back in the seat, starting to relax, when through his accent, the driver revealed his nationality. "*Blease*," he repeated my destination back to me, "Hillel Street." In the mouth of a native Arabic speaker the English "P" turns into a "B."

I froze, managed to mumble "I forgot something!" Then I fled the cab. Half panicking, I accosted the astounded hotel doorman and pleaded with him, "Get me another taxi." I groped for words. "I want a driver with, with . . ." I searched for a euphemism. Finally I blurted it straight out. "Find me an Israeli driver."

Even as I stammered the words, I felt waves of shame rising. I was ushered into the next cab in line, obligingly driven by a Jew.

I kept my eyes focused on the ground, but I felt the dark stare of the Arab upon me as he stood idle beside his idling motor. Humiliation aside, he must have hated me for his lost fare. But however he judged me, it could be no harsher than my own verdict on myself.

My years of so-called liberal convictions hadn't proved strong enough to hold up a feather when it came to reality. I was too chicken to take a ten-minute drive in a registered taxi through western Jerusalem with an Arab driver at eight in the evening. And I was only going from the Hilton to Hillel Street—not from Jenin to Ramallah.

They say a liberal is a bigot who hasn't yet been mugged, but my anxiety anticipated the unthrown stone. Unassisted, I put the dagger in the driver's hand. By my blatant action and blunt words in those brief seconds, I did more damage to the cause of coexistence than I could ever counterbalance by a lifetime of dues to the Association for Civil Rights.

It's no justification protesting that it was the prudent thing to do, an excusable overreaction, that "You never know," or that I have a responsibility to my family as well as my ideals. For when I heard that driver speak and saw his dark eyes in the rear-view mirror, I was light years away from any liberal convictions. When push came to shove, I was handed the opportunity to show where I stood, and I did. I failed the taxi test.

And I am doubly damned. For I know that, presented with the same test, I might again refuse the ride, again feel relief as I got out.

I can no longer whitewash my true colors. I too am a casualty of the occupation and the Intifada it caused—and for that I ask the driver's pardon. I used to just be waiting for peace. Since that abortive ride I am also waiting for my conscience to give me peace.

Chapter Four *Jamal's Wall*

Along with the rest of the world I watched the horror of the terrified Palestinian father and his screaming son cowering from bullets against a stone wall in Gaza. The wall did not protect them. Moments later the wounded father, Jamal al-Durrah, slumped against the stones, cradling the dead boy in his lap.

I recall Jamal beside another wall, one which he had built with his own hands. I pass by Jamal's wall every day. It is in my garden.

I never knew Jamal's last name until his photograph became the tragic logo for the new Intifada in Israel. For all the years of our acquaintance I called him by his first name, and when he finally agreed to talk to me, it was always my first name that he used. Jamal, who had helped build my Israeli house in 1988 and helped maintain it afterward, has been in and out of its rooms many many times. I have never been in his house nor ever seen his children, even though they wore my children's outgrown clothes and played with their discarded toys.

Even if Jamal and I are on a first-name basis, since he is a Palestinian laborer from Gaza and I am a Jewish person living in the suburbs of Tel Aviv, our real lives could intersect only on the most superficial basis. Yet even in the superficiality of my contact with Jamal al-Durrah long before his tragedy became international news, he became exceptional for me.

For three days after I saw the famous footage of September 30, 2000, I had no idea that I knew the victim. Then I read in the newspaper that the dead boy's father, 37 years old, was a house painter from Gaza who worked for Israelis in the suburbs north of Tel Aviv.

The same first name, the same job in the same area, the same general age. Too many coincidences.

I studied the photo more closely. What if . . . ? It was too blurry to see, the angle of the head turned away. To put my suspicions to rest I telephoned Moshe Tammam, the Israeli contractor who had done the work on our home. "Tell me, Moshe, the man in the hospital, that's not our Jamal?"

But the contractor told me what I didn't want to hear.

After his son was killed, Jamal was taken to a hospital in Gaza. Tammam, for whom Jamal has worked for twenty-three years since age 14, telephoned the hospital and urged Jamal to transfer to the Sheba Medical Center, a large public university hospital, in Israel. Tammam promised to cover all the expenses. But instead Jamal was sent to a hospital in Amman, where he was operated on for the eight gunshot wounds in his body.

Tammam says that the Palestinian Authority, eager to keep Jamal a symbol, did not permit his transfer to Israel. Jamal said that he preferred to be treated in an Arab hospital.

Many versions surround the shooting. Like the definition of what is true in the Middle East, facts change depending on whom you talk to. Some preliminary questions arose right away: Whose bullets shot Jamal and his son? What were Jamal and his son doing in the first place in the most dangerous spot in Gaza? Why did the firing keep up during the forty-five minutes they crouched beside the wall? Why did Jamal not cover his son's body with his own to protect him? Did anyone see or hear Jamal's terrified cries for help or his hands raised beseeching them to stop firing? But the hardest question is what the future holds for Jamal al-Durrah, his family, and for all Palestinians and Israelis.

When I talked to Jamal by telephone to his hospital bed four days after he was shot, four days after he became a bereaved parent, the first thing he said when he recognized my voice was to inquire after the health of my husband and children.

I look at Jamal's wall, I remember how I imperiously complained to the contractor when Jamal built it, and I am ashamed of myself and of a wider reality.

I first met Jamal at the height of the first Intifada. In 1988 my husband and I had hired a contractor to renovate an old house we had just bought in an Israeli suburb of Tel Aviv.

Jamal stood apart from the other Palestinian workers. In his 20s, he was angrier, prouder, with a resentment more palpable. We were never really introduced. I just learned his first name over time, and he learned mine.

Tall, thin, and glowering, Jamal spat out his words in low monosyllables. He accepted without a smile, begrudgingly, the cold drinks in paper cups I brought out to the team of workers. The coffee I offered he never would drink. Shaking his head dismissively and clicking his tongue, he would pad silently to the periphery of my unfinished patio, crouch down on his heels, extract a crumpled nylon bag from his jacket pocket and shake some dark granules into a glass cup to brew his own strong coffee over a little portable gas heater.

The other workers in the crew—Nasser, Abed, Jawad, and Yusuf—were unobtrusive. They bent down in my garden to pray, facing east.

As the workers arrived each morning the radio reported the injured of the day before—Israeli soldiers wounded by hurled rocks, Palestinians shot, the tear gas fired, the order from army headquarters to break protestors' limbs, the latest death toll. It was a dark and hateful time. Still the workers came to my house day in and day out, plastering, setting tiles, installing plumbing.

They arrived at dawn, worked quietly, kept their heads down. They considered themselves the lucky ones, the ones with steady work. But when terrorist bombings heated up inside the country, Israel retaliated by sealing off the borders, allowing nobody from the territories occupied by Israel to work inside Israel proper. Sometimes weeks would go by while the men sat in enforced idleness inside Gaza. Then suddenly the order would be rescinded, and construction would start anew.

Part of Jamal's job involved putting up a garden wall. I was walking next to the newly finished wall when something close to the base caught my eye. I bent down to look closer. "Jamal—1988" I saw, inscribed in loping English script letters with the handwriting of a foreign schoolboy.

The cement was already dry. Indignant, I went straight to the contractor and insisted a new layer be spread over the offensive signature. It was my house after all, not a public sidewalk. If anybody had a right to make graffiti, it was me.

The next morning the signature had been obliterated, large circles of new gray cement in benign swirls over the words. The new spot dried a different shade of gray than the surrounding wall, and for a few years your eye could see it if you knew what you were looking for. But with time that difference has faded, and it became hard to discern the place where Jamal had tried to leave his mark.

During the period we were building, my third child was born. I was surprised to hear that Jamal, young as he was, was married and his wife expecting a child. That child would live only 12 years. He was Mohammed.

When I offered Jamal my no-longer-needed maternity clothes, he nodded his head only slightly. I packed up a big bundle including the navy wool jumper I had liked best. The next day I looked until I found

Jamal, and with a smile presented him with the bag. He took it with averted eyes. Months later I found the bag, still full, stuffed into a crevice in an old repainted cupboard, my navy dress in a wrinkled ball.

It was shortly after my house was finished that Jamal, hoping to break the lifetime sentence of working for others, quit his job to open his own shop in Gaza. It was one of Tammam's Jewish workers who told me the story.

The beating came without warning. One morning a group of local Palestinian men swaggered in to Jamal's shop, as if they owned the place, not bothering with even minimal disguise. They beat him with impunity, as if it were their right. As if it were his due.

When they had finished with him, Jamal's broken body was taken to a hospital in Gaza. He was operated on but the operation was not successful. His old Israeli boss Tammam had him transferred at his expense to the orthopedic department of the Sheba Medical Center. That first time, Jamal agreed to go to Israel for treatment. Jamal was treated by a professor of orthopedics and spent months in the hospital. Finally he was discharged, but he cannot yet walk straight, not to this day.

The reason behind the beating has never come to light, at least not to the Israelis Jamal worked beside. Rumor had it that there was a suspicion of drug dealing, or smuggling, or that he was too openly critical of local leadership. Or it might have been revenge on him for a blood feud, for a slight real or imagined, for a violation of the societal code. Whatever the reason, Jamal came out a quarter crippled.

When Jamal recovered, he went back to his old construction job.

Recalling that first terrible injury, Tammam told me, "Jamal will recover this time too. He is a strong, strong man. After the beating he got in Gaza it was a miracle I ever saw Jamal again." But can even as strong a man as Jamal emotionally survive having his son murdered in his own arms?

Tumultuous years went by in Israel. In 1991 there was the acute fear of the Gulf War. In 1993 the Oslo accords brought the first ray of hope for coexistence. But when Prime Minister Rabin was assassinated in 1995 by a Jewish extremist, things seemed to go back to square one. More violence erupted, and then Netanyahu was swept into office.

But in the meantime, people living in the Middle East continued to lead their private lives, maneuvering between the headlines.

A couple of years ago, I hired the same contractor to repaint my house. I saw there was a new foreman. He came up my steps limping slightly, thin and wiry, reminding me of Akhenaton, the Egyptian emperor with the elongated physique. When he got close, I saw it was someone I knew—through the graying hair and bony cheeks I recognized Jamal.

He smiled, and I did too. There was something of old friends in our greeting. I could read in his eyes that I'd gotten older too. I supposed Jamal's traumas had been so much worse than mine, and yet here he was again, after all those years. Years of arising in the middle of the night to take the bus to the border crossing while it was still dark, and then boarding a second bus an hour later out of Gaza to start work at dawn.

Was it this backbreaking cycle of physical labor that made the 35-year-old man look like 50? Yet he was smiling.

I say we greeted as friends, but I know this is not the deeper truth. Even beyond the economic inequality, I could never look at him without "the conflict" on my mind. His Arabness and my Jewishness hung in the air. Scattered carelessly about the house were the tools of builders—axes, power saws, drills, blades, knives. Their potential flitted across my mind. And I wondered: What could I represent for Jamal, in my big house, transplanted to this soil of my own will from another place?

I still brought coffee out to the workers in the morning. This time Jamal looked happy to get it. "But I hope this is real coffee, not Jewish Nescafe!" he would laugh. In his surrender to reality, Jamal had kept both his spunk and his dignity.

Jamal and I conversed in Hebrew, neither his native tongue nor mine. On Fridays he would catch the earlier weekend transport bus to go home. When Jamal called out to me over his shoulder, "A peaceful Sabbath!" I could feel him grinning.

The first coat of paint had to dry and the boss suggested that in the remaining time left before the bus pickup I might ask Jamal to do small jobs needed around the house.

I remembered my university diplomas I had never gotten around to hanging up, and pulled them from the drawer. Holding the frames in his hands, Jamal studied the gothic lettering on one for a long time. "It says *New York University*, right?" he asked finally, his voice serious and hushed. I nodded yes, remembering his painstaking English graffiti, which I had ordered covered up. Jamal hung the diplomas in my study with exquisite care.

There was still time before the bus.

In my youngest daughter's room hangs an old reproduction of Renoir's "Girl with a Watering Can," which had been my own as a child and then passed on like a talisman to each of my three daughters. By now the wooden frame had fallen apart at the hinges. I asked Jamal if he could patch it up somehow.

He nodded. "Do you have any masking tape?"

I foraged in the storage room and came back with a jumbo roll. "Here, take this. It's left over from the Gulf War! Remember when we had to tape up our windows and doors against gas? I guess when I bought this masking tape I thought the war would last longer than it did."

"Allah protect us!" Jamal called with a laugh, holding up the roll. "Imagine how silly we were to think this sticky paper could save our lives.

"Believe me," he went on, "in my house we never taped the windows or the doors. I told my wife, 'If God wants to kill us, he will, and if he wants to save us, he will.' I never put on any gas mask in the war. Never again! Let that be Allah's will," said Jamal.

An hour later he appeared at my study door. He handed me back the roll of tape, still enormous. In his hands he held the Renoir reproduction in a new frame. Looking closer I saw I was mistaken—it was actually the original frame bought halfway across the world at a museum shop decades before. He hadn't used any of the tape at all. On the back Jamal had repaired it by hammering in dozens of tiny nails perfectly lined up all around the edge. Then somehow he had polished the wood to make the black lacquer shine like new.

I asked Jamal how many children he has now.

"Six," he told me proudly. "Four sons, two girls."

This time he didn't hesitate to accept my old clothes and toys, even though I hesitated to offer them. I had learned enough not to hand them to him any more. Now I left the bags in the garden, next to the lamppost where he left his rolled-up jacket when he came to work.

I wished I could help Jamal. I wanted his kids to get enough schooling to read the lettering on their own diplomas.

But he was a victim of circumstances larger than both of us, I rationalized weakly. So I didn't do much of anything. I just stuffed shopping bags full of old sweaters with fuzz balls, men's jackets that had gone out of style, toys my children had gotten tired of, and scuffed boots they had outgrown.

Jamal took them all, every last one. I watched his thin frame receding and saw his limp as he walked down the garden steps. The sinews in his long arms moved as he carried the bulging nylon shopping bags with Hebrew writing down to the boss's pickup truck, in a rush to make the afternoon ride back to Gaza.

The fresh white paint covering Jamal's wall gleamed in the sun. From the western horizon over the beach the afternoon rays shone on the bronze crescent atop the seaside mosque before reflecting in the glass of my windowpanes. Then the light passed eastward, casting its rosy light on Jerusalem, and after that on towards Mecca. Was Jamal watching the fading sunlight too, through the dusty window of his bus?

I wondered whether Jamal would be back when it came time to paint again. Would his hair be all gray then? Would his four sons be old enough to throw stones, or will the time of stone-throwing have passed?

That was a few short years before the Second Intifada, before Jamal had his black moment of fame. It seems a lifetime away.

In 2000, several dozen Jewish families—approximately 400 people—lived in the settlement of Netzarim in the Gaza Strip. According to Israel's Central Bureau of Statistics and to the settlers' organization, the Jewish population of the entire Gaza Strip was 7,000. They were surrounded by almost 1,300,000 Palestinians. Netzarim is an isolated patch of land accessible only on the heavily guarded road that leads from the Netzarim junction, which according to post-Oslo interim agreements is under the jurisdiction and protection of Israeli authorities. One Israeli commander called it "the last eye into Gaza"; for the Foundation for Middle East Peace it was a "wedge between Palestinian population centers," which during the peace process had been transferred to governing by the Palestinian Authority. Jamal lives in the Al Bureij refugee camp founded in 1949 which now has 30,000 inhabitants.

Beginning on the morning of September 30, 2000, Palestinians using rocks, firebombs, and guns attacked Israeli soldiers guarding the junction in an attempt to cut off access to Israeli Netzarim.

There is no doubt that Jamal and his son were caught in the apex of that battle. According to Major General Yom Tov Samia, then head of the Israeli army's southern command, they were part of the attacking crowd, "not there by accident," and as such were under risk. Jamal's employer said that Mohammed was a "problematic, hyperactive boy" and surmised that in all probability he was out there throwing stones. Mohammed's mother Amal has said the boy's nickname was "little troublemaker." According to Tammam, Jamal, hearing where his son had gone, probably rushed over to bring him back home.

Jamal's account is different. In light of Ariel Sharon's symbolic visit to the Temple Mount the previous Wednesday, which had triggered the violence, the Palestinian Authority had declared a general strike on Saturday. So Mohammed, who would normally have gone to his sixth grade class, was home for the day. Jamal had recently sold his 1974 Fiat, and was looking for another car. He was on his way to the used-car auction in Netzarim. "Mohammed was crazy about cars," said Jamal, "I decided to take him with me."

They didn't find a car, and father and son took a taxi back toward their home in Al Bureij. When the cab arrived at the beleaguered Netzarim junction, the driver refused to go further. Jamal and Mohammed got out, and as it seemed quiet at the moment, they decided to cross the junction by foot. Then a barrage of gunfire started and the pair took refuge behind a barrel on the sidelines, against a wall bordering the Palestinian police building.

Detailed diagrams published in the Israeli press and posted on the Web site of the Israel Ministry of Defense show that on one side of Jamal was the Israeli army outpost from which snipers fired. On the building in back of the wall where Jamal leaned and to his other side around the corner of the wall Palestinians were firing at the Israeli outpost. Jamal denied the Israeli version, saying there was no shooting at all coming from the Palestinian direction, so there was no reason for the Israelis to shoot in the direction of Jamal and Mohammed unless they were aiming for them. Palestinian cameraman Talal Abu Rahma, working for France 2 television, filmed the historic footage, and claimed that at first the Palestinians were indeed firing toward the Israelis, but that they "ran away like rabbits after a few minutes."

According to Jamal, he and his son crouched there for forty-five minutes. His son was wounded by one bullet, but was still conscious, and begged his father to save him. Journalist Tom Segev wrote in the newspaper *Haaretz* that the film footage made apparent that Jamal "didn't provide optimal cover for his son. . . . It might have been better had he switched places." Segev interviewed Jamal while he was in the hospital. Why didn't he raise a white cloth to signify surrender? Segev asked. Jamal tearfully replied, "Where would I have got a white cloth?"

Jamal did, however, frantically wave in the direction of the Israeli outpost, shouting in Hebrew. Jamal said, "I cried, 'Stop, stop shooting. You are killing my boy. Stop this insanity.' But they didn't stop. They kept shooting until he was dead." It's doubtful whether Jamal's cries could be heard above the general din. But they could have seen Jamal lifting his arm and pointing supplicating fingers toward the soldiers. Bullets responded, hitting his outstretched arm.

Mohammed was shot early on, but did not lose consciousness. He told his father, "Father, don't be afraid. I can wait for the ambulance to come. I am not afraid."

When Jamal saw that Mohammed was wounded, he used his cell phone to call a cousin. The cousin ordered an ambulance. But the ambulance driver himself was shot dead on the way to evacuate the pair.

The cameraman caught this scene for history. One minute Mohammed is crying, Jamal is shouting, and in the blink of an eye, Mohammed lies dead with a bullet wound in his stomach, and Jamal slumps unconscious against the wall, eight bullet wounds in his elbow, both legs, and right thigh.

Israel did not accept immediate responsibility for the shooting. Instead, it put the blame on the boy for being where he was. "Whoever goes to Netzarim, it's like walking in the rain. You risk getting wet," said Major General Samia. He added that shots were being fired from multiple directions.

But two days later after a preliminary investigation, the Israeli Defense Forces (IDF) apologized for the death, saying that Mohammed was indeed killed by mistaken IDF fire, although the soldiers did not know they were hitting a father and son. Head of the IDF Operation Branch, Major General Giora Eiland, admitted, "This was a grave incident, an event we are all sorry about."

Yet at the press conference when Deputy Chief-of-Staff of the Israeli Defense Forces Major General Moshe Ya'alon called Mohammed's death "heartrending," he reiterated that "the boy had arrived at the spot to throw stones" and insisted that Palestinians were making "cynical use of children" in their attacks on Israelis.

Jamal was adamant that the soldiers aimed specifically at them, which the Israeli army denied. But which soldiers were in the outpost or what the army investigation learned from them has not been revealed. Segev wrote in *Haaretz* that the bullet markings "form a half circle, a kind of halo, which hovers over the place where [Jamal] Duri and his son knelt."

The next day, the Palestinian cameraman Abu Rahma went back to the wall Jamal had leaned on and filmed the bullet markings. In a signed statement under oath the cameraman was unequivocal: "I can confirm that the child was intentionally and in cold blood shot dead and his father injured by the Israeli army." A memorial to Mohammed was put up at the spot shortly after the shooting.

A second ambulance drove the wounded Jamal to a hospital in Gaza City. Moshe Tammam phoned, telling Jamal he had again arranged for him to be treated at the Sheba Medical Center. As he did the previous time, Tammam again offered to foot the bill. It was both Saturday and the Jewish New Year, and so Tammam made his way to the hospital on foot to await Jamal. But Jamal never arrived.

The footage of the tragedy spread quickly, and the King of Jordan offered to have Jamal treated without cost in Jordan. The Jordanian ambassador to Israel flew in and arranged his transfer to the prestigious Hussein Medical Center in Amman. Later Jamal said he called Tammam: "Thank you very much, you are a man of gold, but I cannot offend King Abdullah."

In the hospital Jamal became a celebrity. He was visited by scores of visitors including the Jordanian king, dignitaries, and schoolchildren. Press, radio and television interviews appeared on international and Israeli media.

Only three days after he had lost his son, when the reporter from Israel radio asked Jamal if his attitude toward Israelis changed forever in those terrible moments beside the wall in Gaza, Jamal said, "I am a man of peace. We two peoples must live together. There is no other possibility. There is no other possibility."

But Jamal's first public statement was an angry one. He said, "I hope the world won't forget Mohammed and will avenge his killing by Israel."

His Israeli boss feared that these words would prevent Jamal from getting a security clearance ever again to work in Israel proper. "For Arabs, revenge means forever," said Tammam. "But," he added, "the Talmud says we are not to judge a man in the time of his sorrow."

Tammam himself has had his share of tragedy. "I almost lost my son," says Tammam, "so I know a little bit what Jamal was going through." Several years ago Tammam's 8-year-old son became ill with acute leukemia. When Tammam came home after hearing the news, Jamal was there. He went over to his boss and put his arms around him. The men embraced; both began to cry. Tammam says that moment softened his heart toward Jamal forever. At the Bar Mitzvah celebration of that same recovered son five years later Jamal put on a big black Hasidic hat and danced in a circle with the Jewish men. Few guests suspected Jamal was not Jewish himself.

"These people are born in hatred, raised in hatred," Tammam told me. "They return home from working in big houses to their shacks without even sewage. I can understand them, but don't be under any illusions. They are not our friends. Jamal himself is a terrific man. He has slept in my own home many times. He is a wonderful worker, and I know that I can leave him alone in any customer's house and there will be no theft, no vandalism, no breakage."

Abed and Jawad, Jamal's cousins who also worked for Tammam, accompanied Jamal to the hospital and took Tammam's cell phone with them to Jordan.

I telephoned the hospital in Amman, and when I told Abed who I was, he passed the phone to Jamal. I had prepared for myself a few words of condolence in Arabic, but when Jamal came on the line and I heard his familiar voice, I spoke in Hebrew. When I told him who was speaking, I couldn't believe his response—the first thing he said was to ask about my family.

What about the shooting?

"A crime, a crime" said Jamal. "Forty-five minutes firing without stop. And I cried, 'My son! My son! My son!' but nobody listened. Now he is dead and I am half finished. To shoot at a boy; it's a crime. I hope to be healthy again, but back to work I don't think I will ever be able to go," he said. He called his boss, Moshe, "a brother."

I asked Jamal what does he wish for his remaining children. "My children? To grow as all the children in the world." As we were speaking his voice broke. "That they will be surrounded by all good things and nothing bad, nothing bad."

Some Israelis felt that the army's quick apology was premature—even perhaps mistaken. Within a few weeks of Mohammed's death there were quasi-official Israeli attempts to reconstruct the scenario to examine whether the pair had in fact been shot by Israeli soldiers.

Little more than a week after the shooting Israel destroyed the wall, the barrel, and the adjacent buildings, a security move Major General Samia later called "unintentional." Despite this obstacle, by November 2000 detailed sketches were published showing the location of father and son in relation to the Israeli and Palestinian positions and lines of fire. They still appear on the Web site of the Israel Ministry of Foreign Affairs; the accompanying text states: "The Palestinian boy was apparently hit and killed during the exchange of fire" after Palestinians shot at the army outpost and the soldiers returned fire. The official statement goes on: "The IDF wishes to express its sorrow at the death of the child and at any incident in which lives are lost, but emphasizes that the Palestinians make cynical use of children's lives by sending them to throw stones under cover of Palestinian fire, thus endangering their lives."

Samia, initiating the inquiry as his personal initiative and not at the behest of the army, declared it revealed that "it is quite plausible that the boy was hit by Palestinian bullets in the course of the exchange of fire. . . . The possibility that they were shot by Palestinians is higher than that they were shot by Israelis."

One significant finding related to ballistics analysis of the bullet holes visible in Abu Rahma's video. The Israeli guard post from which bullets were fired was at a 30-degree angle to the wall. Therefore, Samia's experts said, their bullets would have made elliptical holes. However, enlargements of the holes in the wall show round bullet marks, consistent with shots fired straight ahead from behind the cameraman, a location where no Israelis were known to have been stationed or seen. Furthermore, the concrete barrel against which the pair leaned stood between them and the Israeli positions, yet in the photos the barrel showed no bullet marks.

Haaretz called the response to the army's investigation one of "uncontrolled skepticism." But the questions did not go away and reports continued to appear.

For example, in March 2002 the German television network ARD aired a documentary concluding that Mohammed had been killed by Palestinian bullets. Some theories maintained that the entire event may have been staged.

Then in June 2003 the *Atlantic Monthly* published the feature article "Who Shot Mohammed Al-Dura?" Its author, James Fallows, became "convinced" that "the boy cannot have died in the way reported by most of the world's media and fervently believed throughout the Islamic world."

One element upon which Fallows relied was that the video footage aired was an edited version and France 2 television had never released the entire "raw" footage. Charles Enderlin, France 2 Jerusalem bureau chief, replied vigorously in writing to the *Atlantic Monthly*. Enderlin questioned why Fallows did not contact their office while he was in Jerusalem investigating the story. Enderlin maintained that only a few "too unbearable" seconds of the film had been edited out, that there had never been an official Israeli request to provide the raw film material, and that the investigations Fallows cited were undertaken as private initiatives and not at the behest of the Israeli army. "Obviously," Enderlin wrote, "the IDF decided not to conduct any official investigation and preferred not to get involved in a legal procedure which would have necessarily brought independent experts into the picture." The magazine published a much abbreviated version of Enderlin's response.

Jamal himself was adamant: "I am 100% certain that responsibility falls on the Israeli army." He stressed, "I was there, I saw who opened fire . . . [In the Palestinian and Jordanian hospitals] they wrote medical reports that the bullets which injured me are not used by Palestinians. They were the bullets of the Israeli army."

The truth about the death of Mohammed al-Durrah resembles the "truth" of the Middle East—full of contradictions, charges, countercharges, emotional baggage, and polemics. Above all, nothing is neutral.

Millions across the world saw the famous footage. Only a minute fraction were aware of subsequent uncertainties and investigations. Fewer still would have cared or have been convinced by them. Bob Simon of CBS called the picture "one of the most disastrous setbacks Israel has suffered in decades."

In the Arab world the story has no loose ends. The photograph quickly became the icon of the Intifada. Hundreds of parks and schools have been named after Mohammed. The street in Cairo where the Israeli embassy stands has been pointedly renamed Mohammed al-Durrah Street. His face appears on postage stamps and wall posters throughout the Middle East. In 2001 while I was visiting Barcelona I heard news of a suicide bombing in Tel Aviv. I turned to an Arab television station to see if there was coverage; the photo of Jamal and Mohammed was the backdrop screen of the network.

If Mohammed became an icon, Jamal has become a spokesman. His travels have taken him to Iran, Iraq, Morocco, Algeria, Yemen, Saudi Arabia, South Africa, the United Arab Emirates, Jordan, Egypt, and Kuwait. He is hosted by dignitaries and treated with honors, sometimes telling his story on behalf of the cause.

The construction worker has become a public speaker. Jamal, with his innate poise, would do well in the limelight. He also has an exuberance belied by his melancholy exterior. He described with excitement to Tammam the black limousines that chauffeured him through Cairo. When giving interviews about his years in Israel Jamal has boasted of some well-known personalities in whose homes he worked.

Jamal helps bring in public donations, and Tammam believes he has also received personal contributions. There are reports that he received compensation from Saddam Hussein. The *Times* of London reported the family "now financially comfortable, with money, awards and invitations pouring in from Iraq, Iran and other Arab countries eager to fete the first family of the Intifada." The Palestinian Authority pays him a monthly pension. In February 2001 *Haaretz* reported that a check from the Palestinian Authority representing a lump sum payment for Jamal's injuries and for his son Mohammed's death had bounced.

From time to time Jamal has gone to Arab countries to receive further medical treatment for his gunshot wounds. Once in 2003 Israel refused to give him permission to travel to Egypt for treatment, citing "security reasons."

When he is not traveling Jamal returns to his modest home in the Al Bureij camp. In his own community he has become a person of local distinction.

Mohammed's grave bears a large marble headstone, contrasting with smaller ones surrounding it. The inscription reads "This is the tomb of the martyred child Mohammed Jamal al-Durra, murdered September 30, 2000, at the age of 12. To heaven goes your soul, Mohammed." But it is to the site of his son's murder that Jamal returns—when Israeli authorities permit—to place flowers.

The walls outside Jamal's home bear spray-painted images of Mohammed, inside his photograph is displayed. Foreign correspondents still arrive there to interview Jamal and his family.

There was a flurry of renewed interest when Jamal's wife, Amal, gave birth to a boy in November 2002. The parents named him after his dead brother. Interviewed while she was expecting, Amal al-Durrah declared, "I want to revive the name and to tell Sharon and the Israeli soldier who killed him that even if Mohammed died, we can bring more Mohammeds into the world. They can't kill us all." At that time Amal reiterated that although she would "hate Israelis to the Day of Judgment" she would never send her child out to sacrifice himself. Following the birth, however, the Associated Press reported that both parents "said they were prepared to send their other children to die fighting Israel: 'There will be no security for them as long as we have occupation. We're ready to give more of our children.'"

At first Jamal appeared in the Israeli media. In the spring of 2001 an Israeli journalist arranged a meeting in Jordan between Jamal and his wife and an Israeli couple whose 15-year-old daughter had been murdered in the Dizengoff Center suicide bombing in Tel Aviv. A long account of the two couples' emotional encounter was published in *Yedioth Ahronoth*, Israel's largest newspaper. Jamal said, "We have to find a solution. If it will be bad for us, it will also be bad for you. We are too closely tied to each other. Despite what happened to me, I still think there is hope. Give us what you are obligated to under the agreements, and then we can live as good neighbors. I will come to you, and you will come to me. Neither you nor we have another place."

But as time went on I stopped hearing about Jamal in Israel. Since the death of Mohammed, he declared, "I have turned myself into an ambassador to tell the world about our struggle."

How does Tammam react to this? He and Jamal were so close that Jamal was the object of jealousy among the other workers. "They called him Jamal Tammam!" Tammam laughs at the recollection. Jamal spent long periods living in Tammam's house. He helped prepare festive holiday meals and was especially close to Tammam's elderly mother, who was an excellent cook.

In several public statements since the shooting both men called each other "brother." The year after the shooting Tammam said that if Jamal would be in Europe, he would like to travel to see him. But as Jamal's rhetoric hardened, Tammam has grown further away from him. He takes Jamal's anti-Israel statements personally. A note of resentment and betrayal has crept into Tammam's voice. Yet some contact between them persists. Jamal phones Tammam on the eve of holidays. When Tammam's mother passed away, Jamal called to offer his condolences.

Throughout the Intifada Tammam has continued to employ his old Palestinian crew, most of whom are Jamal's cousins. During the long stretches when the border was sealed, Tammam sent them "advances" against their salary. But actually he did not know if they would be permitted to return to work in Israel ever again.

I knew these men since 1988, as I had known Jamal. They were for a time the only Palestinians I ever met. I knew them for years, and they were never anything but polite, hardworking, and kind to my child. They put a human face on that great unknown "the Palestinian," so that afterward when I heard that word mentioned, these men were the ones who came to my mind.

When the border was closed Tammam hired other workers to fill the Palestinians' jobs. His avowed politics are to the right, yet he says he "gave in" and rehired his old Palestinian workers once they could enter again. He could not bear their phone calls begging for work, their pleas that they have no money to feed their kids. "A man has a sense of responsibility," he says, "to people who have spent their lives working for him."

I asked Tammam about Abed and Jawad, who had accompanied the wounded Jamal to the hospital, carrying with them Tammam's cell phone. Entry restrictions are eased from time to time, and when the crossing is open, Jawad comes back. Abed, however, has never been given permission to work in Israel since the Intifada began. For Abed is childless, and permits are only issued to men who have children. Fathers are considered less likely to carry bombs or instigate violence. So Abed has joined the ranks of the 67 percent of other unemployed Gazans.

Once, in a window of time when the border was open, I went to visit Jawad at his work site in an upscale suburb of Tel Aviv.

As I drove up the quiet street lined with white houses and palm trees, I wondered what kind of man would greet me. Would I find him sullen, angry, embittered? And I worried that perhaps he would not have been allowed through, because the previous day a Palestinian attack had claimed fourteen lives in a burning inferno in Israel.

Tammam purposely assigns his Gazan workers to jobs in unoccupied houses. Israelis, he is sure, would be too nervous to have Palestinians around. And surprised friends have warned the contractor himself, "Be careful, you may wind up with a knife in your back."

So it was not without some trepidation that I walked into the garden of the old house surrounded by scaffolding. Skirting the construction debris I walked around to the back, tentatively calling out "Shalom! Shalom!" Finally from the gutted living room a "Shalom" answered back.

The man I came upon was the same man I remembered—chubby and squat, his moon face lit up with a wide smile when he saw me. Jawad Al-Durrah has had only one job in his life: working since he was a teenager for Tammam in Israel. Looking at Jawad with hammer in hand straddling the scaffolding, feeling so lucky to be back at work, an onlooker might be fooled into thinking things hadn't changed. But nothing is the same, not for him or for anybody.

On the job with him was his brother-in-law. They offered me one of the broken chairs in the garden and we talked for half an hour, a three-way conversation in accented Hebrew.

This time they had been back on the job for eight days. Years ago they had to rise at 3 a.m. to get to work by six. Now, they told me matter of factly, their day starts at half past midnight: one and a half hours to the checkpoint by local taxi, then lining up to cross the stages of security checks, revolving doors, body scans, and document verifications. For fear of bomb smuggling, they are not permitted to carry anything, not even lunch. By a quarter to four they are on the Israeli side where a bus carries them to a main intersection in the heart of the country. At 5 a.m. they alight, and walk the two miles through the dark to the work site where they await the arrival of the boss at dawn. Then, five hours after waking up, they start work. That was the situation when we met in 2002.

By the spring of 2004 work permits allowed the workers to stay overnight in Israel, so they remained on the job from Sunday to Friday, and needed to make the grueling journey only twice a week. But in May new violence at the Erez checkpoint, where Gaza meets Israel, caused Israel once again to seal off that crossing, only to reopen it a month later. That's the way it has gone during the Intifada years: open, closed, open, closed.

When I asked the men about their children, whether they also throw stones, they protested animatedly, "Our sons? If we hear they went to throw stones, we would beat them! The fathers who don't care, their sons go stone throwing. But we are worried—so we hit our sons!"

Every day after school, they related, boys divide into two groups: those who sneak out to throw stones through cuts they make in the barbed wire dividing the refugee camps from the Israeli settlements, and the others who are afraid of their parents and go straight home to study. Since our meeting the area between the camp and the settlements was razed by the army, making these kind of forays impossible in any event.

Their boys are the cousins of Mohammed al-Durrah. But his tragic example and the continuing stream of killed and wounded children haven't made them want to miss the action. When the Israeli planes roar outside, the children run to look out the windows.

And what about Jamal? I asked. He will never be allowed back in Israel, his cousins said. And besides, he is not fit for work anymore.

What will he do for the rest of his life?

"The rest of his life?" they repeated, as if the future is a foreign concept. And they shrugged.

Half a year after the shooting Jamal was a guest on a popular Israeli interview program. Obviously unable to come into Israel to the studio,

Jamal was interviewed from his home in the refugee camp. He repeated the story he has told over and over about the forty-five minutes he was pinned with his son beside the barrel being shot at. Jamal broke down telling the story. Tammam told me that during that first year a lot of their time on the phone was spent with Jamal weeping.

A Jewish settler in Gaza, Noga Cohen, appeared on the same interview program. Three of Noga's children were injured in a bomb thrown into their school bus in November 2000. Her 7-year-old son lost a leg, her 12-year-old daughter lost a foot. Another daughter, 8 years old, was sent to intensive care where doctors tried to save at least one of her legs. Their efforts failed. Both legs had to be amputated.

The interviewer switched back and forth between Jamal and Noga. After Noga had told her story, he asked Jamal if he could identify with her.

"Yes," Jamal said. "Of course. Human beings are not walls."

So it all came back again to a wall: all the walls Jamal built and painted for Israelis since he was 14 years old. The wall he flattened himself against with Mohammed trying to escape the bullets, the wall that didn't protect them. And finally, Jamal's wall in my garden, his name erased but standing out in my mind more prominently than ever.

Chapter Five   *A Perfect Day for a Swim*

During the first spring of the new millennium Pope John Paul II paid an historic visit to Israel. One of his key stops was the Mount of the Beatitudes beside the Sea of Galilee. The pope spoke on the same site where Jesus had delivered the most famous love address of all time— the Sermon on the Mount.

Unfortunately, the pope's visit coincided with days of heavy rain. And in Israel rainfall, like so much else, is never temperate. Either a dry spell stretches on for weeks and months, lowering the reservoirs beneath the red line and prompting drought alerts, or the heavens open up delivering deluges that bear an uncanny resemblance to the story of Noah.

The Hebrew language has no word for drizzle. When the rains come, the temperature plummets, the wind whips up, and the drops pelt down in angry streams through city streets and especially over the rocky terrain of the Galilee.

It had been pouring for days before the pope's visit, and by the time he arrived at the Mount of Beatitudes the whole area was a mass of mud. The thousands of Christian pilgrims from around the world who had traveled to Jesus' hill suffered through cold wet hours in order to catch a glimpse of the Holy Father.

For as bestially hot as the Holy Land is in the summer, the bone cold of the winter is an untoward shock. During World War One an unprepared British soldier in the campaign to oust the Turks from their 700-year control of the Holy Land dismally compared the Judean hills to the Himalayas. In 2000 the soggy international multitude huddled under ineffective umbrellas to hear the pope's message of peace.

Pope John Paul visited the Holy Land just half a year before the Intifada thunder bolted the Middle East. Perhaps the stormy heavens over the Mount of Beatitudes in the spring of 2000 were a sign that the sunshine of seeming peace would be short lived and that endless unpleasant days lurked just around the bend.

From the gentle mount where Jesus delivered his sermon one can look down and see spread southward at one's feet the famous Sea of Galilee. It was here that Jesus is said to have fed the multitudes with one fish and a loaf of bread, and it was upon these waters the New Testament reports Jesus to have walked. Jews have inhabited the area since biblical times, the area was a Roman province and occupied by the Crusaders. The city on its shores bears the name of the Roman emperor Tiberias.

The name on English maps is actually a gross misnomer, for the Sea of Galilee is no sea at all. Known in Hebrew as the Kinneret, the Sea of Galilee is Israel's only fresh water lake. By North American standards it is a modest body of water, thirteen miles long and eight miles wide. But perhaps because it is unique, Israelis are unduly proud of the patch of water whose blue becomes breathtakingly visible from the high road shortly after passing Mount Tabor on the two-hour drive from Tel Aviv. In the early 1900s, Rachel Bluestein, one of Israel's first poets to write in the newly revived Hebrew language, wrote a poignant ode to the lake called "My Kinneret." Bluestein was so famous and admired that until today she is known simply as "Rachel." Rachel's poem was set to melancholy music, to become of the best loved Hebrew folk songs. It is one of the standards played by Israel radio on one of its numerous days of mourning—after a terrorist attack while waiting for the casualty details to come in, or on a day of multiple funerals of victims.

Since the beginning of the renewed Jewish settlement of Palestine, the Kinneret has also served as a place for holiday visits. In the early days when overseas travel was a rarity, Tiberias was a fashionable wintertime spot for the vacationing bourgeois. Although northerly, it lies 682 feet below sea level and thus enjoys a temperate wintertime climate. In summer it is correspondingly hotter than many other parts of the country. The unrivaled matriarch of hotels was the luxurious Galei Kinneret, which boasted of playing host to David Ben-Gurion, Konrad Adenauer, and Danny Kaye among its famous guests.

I have a photo of myself swimming in the Kinneret during my first visit to Israel at age 10. My wet head bobs in the blue background, swimming the sidestroke, a stroke as outmoded in the swimming world as sidesaddle is in the world of riding. Supervised child of summer camp that I was, I was shocked that here I could swim out as far as I liked, not watched by any lifeguard, with no buddy to keep an eye on me. The Kinneret in April was warmer than a Maine lake in late July.

During the traditional holiday weeks of Sukkoth in autumn and Passover in spring, the lake used to be dotted with families who arrived to camp around its shores. They would pitch tents, cook their meals on portable barbecues, and hang their wet suits to dry on the branches of the eucalyptus trees.

Shortly after we arrived to live in Israel we too went on an overnight camping trip with an Israeli family. Told it was to be a picnic, I arrived with packed hard-boiled eggs and cheese sandwiches. When suppertime came the other couple set up a folded table upon which they piled up plastic containers filled with hand-cut salads, cold chicken cutlets, fruits, and homemade cakes. From picnic hampers they produced cardboard salt and pepper shakers. The coup de grace was their checked oilcloth tablecloth. My cheese sandwiches were less than a pathetic contribution. They laughed good-naturedly at an American who clearly had no inkling of what de rigueur Israeli camping was all about. But I felt embarrassed nonetheless, as I often did when trying to blend in with Israeli customs. Israelis would be surprised that I could feel something approaching humiliation, for it was certainly not their intention to make me feel that.

On the shores of the Kinneret I underwent a scenario played out many times to come in my social life in Israel: my customs and background were unused, overlooked, unasked. So I sat by myself beside the water, conjuring up past camping trips in New England: the portaging of the canoes from lake to lake, the feeling of skimming over a mirror surface at sunrise, the tangled water lilies through which we paddled in July, the pine trees darkening to black after the sun set. I squinted, trying to view the Kinneret as a lakeshore in Maine, but the fantasy just wouldn't stick.

Over the years the popularity of the Kinneret declined with the corresponding rise in foreign travel. When Israel conquered the Sinai Desert in 1967, many campers deserted the Sea of Galilee to descend in the thousands upon the pristine Red Sea. When Israel handed back that territory to Egypt in 1982 the Sinai lost some of its appeal, but Israelis never returned in force to the Kinneret. Yet the western coast of the Sea of Galilee is still ringed with several high-rise hotels built in the 1970s through the 1990s by entrepreneurs hoping for a renaissance that has never materialized.

From far away the city of Tiberias looks picturesque. The closer one gets the shabbier it appears. It is a town that never succeeded in pulling itself out of provincial doldrums, its streets crowded with unappealing stores, the smell of fried oil hanging in the air. The crowd appears shabby, unfashionable, a peripheral mix of laborers, unsophisticated merchants, and new immigrants still wearing greenhorn's clothes, caught up in difficult lives. Not much of an introduction to a resort.

Even the lakeside restaurants lack the charm of similar establishments elsewhere in the Mediterranean. The red tablecloths are often
spotted with grease. Fishermen still ply the lake, as they did in Jesus'
day, even though there are periodic scares that the waters are polluted
and the fish have absorbed their unhealthy residues.

The winds work against Tiberias. In the morning, the lake often
looks glasslike and pristine. But by noon the wind usually rises, blowing westerly and making boating, waterskiing, or even sunbathing
unappealing. On cold days, the wind is sharp, and on hot ones, it seems
to consist of blasts from inside a turbo oven.

Yet if the city on the lake's western shore is a place that success seems
to have eluded, its people have a small town friendliness absent from brash
Tel Aviv. They say good morning, and have the time to look one another
in the eye. And here, too, are jewels to be discovered, like the Church of
Saint Peter almost hidden from view until accessed from the lakeside
promenade. Built by the Crusaders in the shape of a boat in honor of its
famous namesake, the church is still in regular use after 900 years.

The southern shore of the lake is ringed by collective farms that
till the fertile land. Thousands of banana trees grow, their fruit wrapped
in blue plastic bags to ward off birds and insects.

Until 1967 only the thinnest strip of land on the eastern shore of
the lake was under Israeli control. Kibbutzim were established to create
a permanent Jewish presence, like Ein Gev founded in 1937. Less than
a mile away stood the Syrian border. Above the shoreline rises the steep
plateau of the Golan Heights. It was from these heights that for decades Syrian gunners would take aim and shoot at the farmers in the
kibbutzim below. When Israel won the Six-Day War in June 1967, the
Golan was one of the territories it conquered. No more, it said, would
its farmers be threatened by the Arab gunners.

Israel thereafter expanded its no longer beleaguered settlements on
the eastern shore of the lake. Near Kibbutz Ein Gev a water park
opened up in the 1980s. For Israeli children it was an irresistible at-
traction. In May 1987 for my middle daughter's 11th birthday we drove

her, her sister, and two friends all the way up to that water park, over three hours each way. They slid down the giant slides unaware of the place's bloody history of battles and conquests.

The Kinneret passed out of our lives, and a long time went by before I found myself going back. But when my youngest daughter joined a swim team in the third grade, I found myself at the lakeside again each September on the day of the annual event attended by swimmers from all over Israel.

Early September 2000, a few weeks before the Intifada broke out, was no exception. At the same time as ten swimmers on the Israeli Olympic team were putting in their final tense practice sessions for the summer Olympics in Sydney, Australia, their next-generation heirs back home were taking part in the laid-back forty-seventh annual swim across the Sea of Galilee.

Thousands converged from around the country—Jewish children from Jerusalem and faraway Beersheba, alongside Arab boys and girls from the Galilee, and a guest delegation of swimmers from the Palestinian Authority. If it cannot be said that the Arab and Jewish children actively mingled with each other, it is true that they swam together and then lounged peaceably side by side on the grass.

When they entered the water at 8 a.m. the mist was still on the horizon and the lake a mirror. As they emerged two or three hours later to the claps of waiting parents and coaches, the sky had cleared and the sun beat hot on the aquamarine surface, on the date palms growing near the shoreline, on the winding road that leads across the nearby mouth of the Jordan River, and on toward the Hashemite Kingdom of Jordan. It was a day of flags and smiles and ice cream, a perfect day for a swim.

The event was a happening, not a race. There was a short course for beginners and a longer trajectory for stronger swimmers. Everyone who finished received a certificate, chocolate milk, and a sandwich. Music played. Games were organized afterward on the shore, and some parents took part beside their children.

Companies sent delegations. Older swimmers who re-swam the course they first did decades ago were honored. Nevertheless, it was an unspoken given that the day, like the future, belonged to the kids.

Crossing the Sea of Galilee is a lark compared to the swimmers' usual grueling workouts. From the age when they first display their talent and motivation, children on swim teams practice almost daily, spending twenty hours a week and more in lap after endless lap. Their lives are surrounded by chlorine, their routines bounded by goggles and flippers. Success is measured in fractions of seconds.

Countless hours in the water are directed toward one pinnacle of achievement: to be part of the Israeli Olympic team, the one on which in 2000 forty Israeli athletes had their shot at glory. In this they are no different from the thousands of other young athletes with the same dream practicing day in and day out in Pasadena, Bangor, Helsinki, and Lyon.

But for Israeli athletes there is one crucial difference. The Arab–Israeli conflict intrudes here too. That difference was indelibly sealed with the murder of eleven Israeli Olympians at the hands of Palestinian Black September terrorists during the 1972 games in Munich. The terrorists surprised them in their rooms in the Olympic Village and took them hostage. The standoff with the authorities ended in their deaths.

I had watched the bloody denouement of Munich on television in New York. Recently I was reminded of the experience in a most un-likely place: a watch repair shop in Tel Aviv. While the burly watch-maker sat hunched on his stool and peered at my watch through his eyepiece, I glanced at a fading reprint from a 1996 *People* magazine on the wall of his narrow store. Henry Herscovici, who greeted me in a Hungarian accent with a smile and a twinkle in his eye, had been a competitor in rifle shooting on the Israeli team in Munich in 1972. By lucky chance, he had been in a room overlooked by the terrorists. As always, I was stunned to meet someone in prosaic circumstances who has had a brush with history. Israelis take these meetings more in stride. "It's a small country," they say.

Ever since Munich, every delegation of Israeli youths to go abroad to any sports event or other official trip worldwide receives a pre-departure security briefing by experts. They learn what to do if they get separated from their group, how to keep an extra watchful eye on their belongings lest an explosive be slipped inside, to make sure anything they buy is wrapped in their presence, not to wear clothes with Hebrew logos. In short, if not to hide their nationality, not to wave it around either.

Children, especially athletes, believe they are invincible. Yet for Israeli parents sending their offspring abroad, Munich is always at the back of their minds. How early should children be told of the risks, risks for which they must consciously prepare as part and parcel of their citizenship? Sport is about youth, freedom, empowerment, joy, achievement, discipline. But in the modern world it can also be about fear.

In the 2000 Sydney Olympics a plaque was erected commemorating the eleven Israeli victims in Munich. It bore their names and, somewhat ironically, the biblical words, "They were swifter than eagles and stronger than lions."

Meanwhile, the Jewish and Muslim girls and boys back in Israel emerged from the Sea of Galilee at the finish point breathless, dripping, and innocent. In all probability they were unaware that on a hill overlooking the same lake Jesus had preached, "Blessed are the pure in heart."

Resting on the grass, each swimmer put on the T-shirt bearing the logo of his local team. With a few thousand more hours of practice and a dose of luck, some might have the fortune to wear the blue and white warm-up suit of the Israeli Olympians four, eight, or twelve years down the line. By then maybe the times they clocked in butterfly and freestyle would be all they would have to worry about. In September 2000 that seemed not too much to hope for.

But by the next September, for the forty-eighth annual swim across the Sea of Galilee, things had undergone a sea change.

At 13, my daughter had just moved up to the senior swim team, which planned to arrive at the Kinneret the night before the swim for an overnight in sleeping bags. As the team's youngest member, my daughter talked excitedly of going to the swim and camping with the "big kids."

But September 2001, eleven and a half months after the Intifada broke out, was a different world. Tourism had fallen 90 percent and the hotels in Tiberias were ghost towns. The owners of the Galei Kinneret tried valiantly to keep it on, but in the winter of 2001 that landmark, too, shut its doors, managing to reopen in 2003. The trickle of violence had become a steady stream and hardly a day went by without a victim. By evening the morning's casualties were often old news.

My husband and I anxiously discussed what to do. Should we decline to let our daughter go when all her friends would be there? Would we be overreacting to think that keeping her close to home was to keep her safe?

After all, nowhere in Israel was safe anymore. The town of Netanya, which has seen repeated suicide attacks, is only twenty minutes straight up the highway from us, and Tel Aviv, where a score of teenagers were killed in a discotheque blast in June 2001, is the same distance in the opposite direction.

Still, some situations are more secure than others, and not just because of a mental attitude. To reach the Sea of Galilee, our team would travel through roads that cut solidly past Israeli-Arab towns and villages, where there had been numerous stone throwings and lethal shootings at passing cars.

Most dangerous of all was to be out in the open among a large crowd—exactly the scene at the swim. Imagining our daughter on an exposed beach milling among thousands of people that no security guards could possibly hope to check—the thought sent shivers down our spine.

With heavy hearts we decided to defer dealing with the permission slip until talking to the coach.

I called with a list of questions prepared. But the coach stopped me short: "I've pulled our team out. This is an extraordinary situation. It's not a time for trips."

The forty-eighth swim across the Sea of Galilee took place as scheduled, but minus the attendance of the Herzliya swim team and many others. A swimming outing was another casualty of "The Situation."

By the next fall, 2002, the violence and danger continued, but perhaps we had grown accustomed to it. Before we had been afraid of stone throwings on the Wadi Ara road, but that same road through which the bus had to travel had seen buses blown up in the year that passed.

So when the time for the swim approached, I didn't consider not sending my daughter out with the rest of the team. The swim went on, although the Israeli-Arab presence was muted, and of course no delegates from the Palestinian Authority were there. We just kept our fingers crossed when she went out on the bus in the early morning that her team would not become a statistic, would not be the unlucky bus to be sabotaged by bombers.

It was just a little over two years since the pope had delivered his message of optimism on the Mount of the Beatitudes. But in Israel that already seemed like a distant irrelevant dream.

Chapter Six

The Routine of Catastrophe:
Of Seeing-Eye Dogs and My Husband's Gun

June 11, 2002: A bomb close to home.

It is 7:45 p.m. and I am on the tennis court in Herzliya playing in the cool of evening. On the next court a teenager races from side to side hitting the ball hard, her ponytail bouncing. As I watch her, wondering what she thinks of our middle-aged match, the girl's cell phone rings.

She speaks into it, and her face changes. She blurts across to our court: "There's been a terrorist hit!" A bombing these days has become no more unusual than cell phones ringing on tennis courts. But then she adds, "In Herzliya."

A second later her phone rings again. "It's in the center of town, next to where they used to have the department store." My partner and I know exactly where she means.

It is minutes after the bomb exploded, details are still sketchy, and casualty figures haven't yet been announced.

We stand stock still on the court and click off in our minds where each one in our family is at that moment. I am not worried for mine; I know nobody could be on that corner. But I rush to make a hurried call to my mother just to let her know I am safe.

My tennis partner runs to her bag and pulls out her mobile phone, tries to dial her elderly parents; they live in the center of town in the vicinity of the blast and often take evening strolls. But it is useless—the lines are all jammed. The phone just beeps busy. As soon as a bomb explodes, thousands of callers are simultaneously trying to get through, to check as my friend is doing.

We are about three miles from the explosion, but soon we too hear the sirens and see an unmarked police car racing down the road, wailing.

Nothing big has ever happened here before. Although Netanya is just fifteen minutes away, and Kfar Saba the same distance—both the sites of too many lethal attacks—it seems almost as if they are a different world. We have never been in the unhappy headlines.

I've argued with my teenage daughter when she wants to go to the mall. "But Mom, no bomb ever goes off in Herzliya," she pleads with me. And sometimes I give in. We have talked ourselves into the fantasy that our Herzliya is somehow safe.

My partner and I continue to play, but distractedly. We finish early and race home to watch the news. There on CNN is the unremarkable street where we go to do our errands. An hour after the attack, it is still swarming with ambulances and police.

Suddenly, after so many casualties, it is this evening's explosion that brings catastrophe to the fore. Like not really believing we are mortal until death claims someone close to us, it took the bomb in Herzliya to make me see myself in danger.

The attack turns out to be a minor one in the grand scheme of things. First reports list only one fatality, the bomber himself. They say his explosive did not detonate properly. Twelve are wounded, but only one seriously, a young girl. Only one seriously, we say, relieved, as if her wounds didn't count.

There were other attacks around the country that day, with several wounded. But when you see a restaurant you have passed a thousand times turn into a burnt-out gutted shell, and blood on a sidewalk you've walked, and when describing it you say, "It's right across the street from that little store where I always bought the children's shoes," that's when violence is suddenly no longer theoretical.

Later the reports are updated. The girl in the restaurant dies of her wounds. She was 15. Maybe when she wanted to go out and do regular teenage things she too used to assure her mother, "But Mom, no bomb ever goes off in Herzliya."

Herzliya has been quiet ever since. The broken glass was carted off, the blood wiped away, and the next day the street where the bomb exploded looked exactly as it always had. My daughter and her friends responded with shock, but after a short time they returned to normal. They again congregate at the Herzliya mall in their free time to meet friends, eat pizza, see a movie, search for interesting T-shirts, or wander around like teenagers do everywhere. After all, she points out, the explosion occurred not at the mall but on a public street. The security at the mall is very tight, she tells me, and when I drive her there I see that she is right. The entrance has been cordoned off into a sort of no-man's-land ten feet square. The armed guards check all entrants far away from the originally constructed door, rummaging into purses and patting down bodies. Still, when I drop her off, I never feel relieved until she is back home, and I myself almost never go to the mall, even though it might otherwise have been a convenient place to shop.

The older my child grows, the harder it will get to plan for her security. Luckily, she walks to school, so the anxiety of public buses does not enter into our picture. But living in this artificially protected bubble narrows her life exposure. She is deprived of the normal growing-up experience of discovering new neighborhoods and mingling with a cross section of people while riding public transportation. The Intifada has contributed to a monochromatic life.

But no parent can forbid a 19- or 20-year-old from going to cafés, pubs, discotheques, rock concerts, or the beach. Often a throng is precisely where adolescents long to be.

At the late-night jam session at Mike's Place on the Tel Aviv beachside on a spring night in 2003, a bomber killed three people: a middle-aged musician, and two patrons in their 20s. One was an immigrant from France whose body was then shipped back to her parents for burial. She was not the first young person who came to Israel for a new life and ended in an El Al plane inside a coffin. The pub's owner stood wrapped in a blanket, crying. "One of the waitresses lost an arm but she's still alive," he said. But young people usually feel invincible, so if they are more shocked when one of them is cut down, they also seemingly rebound faster.

A few weeks after the bomb I slowed down my car as I drove by the reopened Mike's Place. The tables were invitingly set on the sidewalk, and a sign announced upcoming music performers. In front, though, was a heap of cellophane-wrapped flower bouquets wilting in the sun, memorial flowers placed by mourners. Every bomb site has them for a while. Mike's Place is directly adjacent to the garage entrance at the back of the American embassy. I tried to look innocent as the vigilant embassy security guard caught me staring, trying to read the message on a wreath with its greeting written in French. The car in back of me started to beep impatiently, and I drove away.

The community where I live, Kfar Shmariahu, is a separate small town distinct from the adjacent larger Herzliya. It is a tight-knit residential suburb of about 3000 residents that has only four possible roads leading in and out. Late in the spring of 2002 we noticed two little wooden booths going up: one at a one-way entrance road, the other at the one-way exit. Because of the rash of terrorist attacks, the town had decided to impose its own new measures. Between midnight and 6 a.m. two of the entry roads are now closed off by gates. Starting at 10 p.m. the two remaining roads have armed guards posted all through the night. Every car that approaches is directed to slow down and pass by the guard, who peers inside, then waves the car on. Town residents can attach stickers to their windshields, and then the guard's glance is but a cursory one.

Every time I come across this blockade I am surprised anew. The guard is friendly; he smiles and waves me through. But I don't ever pass without a sinking feeling. It reminds me of the gated communities I saw in other parts of the world, where rich residents seal themselves off from the locals. And I recall stories of dangerous places like Nigeria, where foreign diplomats have gates lowered at night upon the staircases inside their homes, sealing themselves off in their bedrooms from intruders who may break in downstairs.

Although the reason is for security, town residents are happy that a by-product has been a decrease in home and automobile burglaries. In the beginning I was very shocked, but as time passes it shocks me less. It is not that hard to get used to living in a golden cage, especially when the door remains open for me.

The checkpoints at the gates of my town are repetitions of what is encountered in every place in this society. Ours is a life where armed guards are part of the fabric, as endemic as traffic lights, door locks, telephone booths, bus stops, butcher shops, and dentists. What by rights should be glaringly abnormal has become routine.

My cardiologist husband works until mid-afternoon at a teaching hospital. As is common among Israeli physicians, he begins his private practice later in the afternoon, seeing patients into the evening. On March 4, 1996, his first patient was scheduled for five in the afternoon. Having finished his hospital work early, he happily saw that he had an hour to spare, enough time to go to the optician and fill the prescription for new glasses that he had been carrying around for weeks but hadn't managed to get around to. At that time his office was on Dizengoff Street in Tel Aviv. The optician was within walking distance of his office, on the second floor of an urban mall called Dizengoff Center. He calculated he would just have enough time to park near his office, walk to the mall, and be back in time for the patient.

But as he was about to leave the hospital, his phone rang. It was his five o'clock patient. Would he, she wondered, be willing to see her at four instead? Why, he asked. She responded apologetically: she hadn't realized when she made her appointment that tonight was the first night of Purim. She wanted to attend holiday services at the synagogue, but if her appointment was at five she would be too late. My husband is not religiously observant, but he could hear in her voice that the holiday was important to her, and he knew that the woman's health was such that it was best for him to see her that day.

He calculated that he could see the patient at four, and then have a free hour between five and six to walk to the opticians before his next appointment. It wasn't the most convenient thing to have to arrive at his office, leave, and then go back, but he agreed.

At 4:04 p.m., just as my husband arrived at his office, exactly at the time he had originally been planning to arrive at the opticians, one of the deadliest suicide bombs in Israel up to that time went off at the entrance to the Dizengoff Center mall. A young Palestinian with explosives strapped to his body had tried to get into the mall, but was turned away by the guard in front, who thought he looked suspicious. He immediately detonated his nail-studded bomb, killing himself and causing mayhem around him.

Bodies lay strewn around the sidewalk. The dead were covered with makeshift black plastic garbage bags. Dozens of ambulances screamed their way to the location.

When the count was finished, thirteen had been killed and over a hundred injured. One who lay dead was a mother who had taken her bride-to-be daughter into town for a wedding dress fitting. The bride was not killed, but her grandmother who accompanied them was. Another three victims were 15-year-old high school girls—three friends on school holiday because of Purim. They lived an hour north of Tel Aviv in a town called Tel Mond, and had taken the bus still wearing the makeup and costumes they had put on for Purim. Near the girls' homes in Tel Mond there is a memorial to their memories in a small grove with three palm trees growing one next to the other. The parents of one of the girls, Bat Chen Shahak, were the bereaved couple who met with Jamal and Amal al-Durrah in Jordan.

Minutes after the blast, I heard the news on the radio. Since the beginning of the Intifada, I switch on the radio dozens of times a day to hear of any new emergency. The Dizengoff Center blast happened in 1996. But terrorist bombing wasn't new to the Intifada. A Supersol supermarket in Jerusalem was the location of one of the first terrorist bombs all the way back in 1969. That supermarket still exists, and I never pass it without thinking of that unwelcome notoriety. Attacks have come in waves since then, and it would be impossible to remember all the locations, except for particularly shocking lethal incidents. In the months following Yitzhak Rabin's assassination in November 1995 there was a resurgence of these attacks. By March 1996 I was already used to turning on the radio for bad news.

I knew of my husband's plans to go to the opticians that afternoon, but not of his change in schedule. When I heard what had happened I was stiff with fear. It was in the days before we had cell phones. There was no answer at his hospital. When I tried to phone his office the receiver just beeped a high-pitched busy signal. This is not unusual after attacks. Everybody with any connection to the location immediately begins phoning, so that the telephone lines became overloaded and jammed. I waited in terror until the phone rang, and heard my husband's voice telling me about the miracle coincidence that had saved him.

I was unable to move, or to read, cook, or work, and I couldn't bear to watch TV and see the volunteers combing through the blood-stained rubble for body parts. I am not a religious person; I hardly ever go to synagogue. But on that black afternoon, I felt myself drawn to the Purim services being held in the town synagogue near my house. The rabbi said it was not a day to sing the traditional joyous songs of that holiday. Instead there would just be the reading of the scroll of Esther, the story of how the Jewish people in ancient times had been saved on Purim from a plan to annihilate them. The packages of candies traditionally prepared for children on Purim were handed out minus the usual festivities, and then I and the rest of the congregation silently filed out and returned home.

Accounts like my husband's near miss at Dizengoff Center are not unusual. Many people I know can tell of a similar experience. They recount how a child, parent, or friend was due to be at some site where a bomb went off, and, by the luck of circumstance, missed being there. They didn't catch the bus they wanted, they overslept, they woke up sick, their appointment was canceled, they were delayed, they changed their mind at the last minute. Even the non-superstitious have the uncanny feeling that some unseen hand intervened to keep them alive. Years after that bomb, hearing American-Israeli poet Karen Alkalay-Gut recite her poem "Almost" at a poetry reading, confirmed that my husband's near miss and my reaction to it were far from unique:

> Everyone I know just missed
> being blown up at five to four on Monday.
> Every one I know just turned
> the corner and looked back
> when it blew up, or took
> a different route that day
> and were a few blocks
> off. Only a few
> were supposed to be elsewhere
> but missed the bus, or the light, or their luck,
> and wound up all over Dizengoff.

Fate has not been kind to unlucky hundreds. Since the Intifada started there have been so many bombings that it is impossible to keep them straight. But every person has some incidents that shocked him in a special way, picking up on an arbitrary poignant detail that in his mind comes to represent the senseless slaughter of innocents.

An 11-year-old Ethiopian girl confided to her classmates her daily fear that the bus she boarded every morning to get to her sixth grade class might blow up. She was the daughter of hotel workers unemployed because of the drop in tourism. They had no money to pay for taxis for their frightened daughter. Her parents were due to leave the country the following month to try to get work in the United States, but in June 2002 their little girl was killed on the Jerusalem bus she was taking to school. Her fearful classmates waited and waited for her to come in and take her seat, but she never showed up.

Another passenger was a 70-year-old retired chiropractor; every Tuesday he volunteered to treat crippled children in a rehabilitation hospital. He said he picked Tuesdays because according to Jewish tradition that day is "doubly blessed." It was the last Tuesday of his life.

Another killed on the bus was Iman Kabha, a 25-year-old Arab student at David Yellin Teachers' College in Jerusalem. For hours after the bus blew up his frantic friends combed the area, calling Iman's cell phone, which rang on unanswered. His body was finally identified as one of the eleven dead.

Kabha came from the Palestinian village of Barta'a in the lower Galilee. His village has the dubious distinction of having been arbitrarily cut in half after the War of Independence. In 1949, when the international boundaries were being drawn, some diplomat drew the line through what turned out to be the center of Barta'a, so that for decades half the town was in Israel and the other half in Jordan. Because the two countries were in a state of belligerency, families were separated for nearly twenty years. They would gather at the border and call out news to each other: so-and-so had been married, so-and-so had had a son. In 1967, after the Six-Day War, the village was in some way reunited. There was no more physical separation between the two sides, but one half still remained formally part of the territories occupied by Israel, and its residents enjoyed neither Israeli citizenship nor the coveted right to work in Israel. The Israeli half of Barta'a continued to be richer, more developed, and the object of envy among the residents of the Palestinian half.

Over 200 of his fellow students made their sad way from Jerusalem for Kabha's funeral. His father addressed the young people sitting assembled before him. "I do not know which of you is Jewish and which Arab," he said, "but I thank you all for coming to honor my son."

These are the kinds of stories that I hear on the radio day in and day out, the terrible tragedy of lives randomly cut short, of people mutilated, side by side with corresponding tales of bravery, caring, and help.

I know the second I switch on the radio if there has been an attack— I hear screaming ambulances in the background, disjointed nervous reports by news people switching back and forth between the scene and the hospitals and updating the information as it comes in piecemeal minute by minute, preliminary reports by police, rescuers, and eyewitnesses. I can guess the general location by the names of the hospitals. If Shaare Zedek and Hadassah are mentioned, it means it happened in or around Jerusalem. Ichilov, Tel-Hashomer, and Wolfson mean Tel Aviv. Meir means Kfar Saba. Laniado means Netanya. Rambam means Haifa. Afula means north. Soroka means south.

Regular broadcasts are suspended for hours. The same sickening scenes play themselves out in the media time and again: casualty estimates, then mortality and injury figures, the names of the dead released as they are identified by the forensic institute at Abu Kabir. Sometimes days go by before all names are released, until after family members have been found and privately informed. Then the following day shots of multiple funerals, of crying relatives, of eulogies, the photographs and brief biographies of the dead and the death announcements in the newspapers. After one Jerusalem bomb, high school students went from funeral to funeral of their classmates at the same cemetery on the same afternoon. More and more now, as victims turn out to be new immigrants, foreign workers, or tourists, their caskets are borne to the airport to be sent for burial close to their relatives in the land of their birth.

I know it all by heart, sometimes I vow not to watch or read about it yet again, but usually I, like many others, am mesmerized nevertheless. It is a relentless scenario that makes my stomach want to turn, that makes me shake my head with helplessness and grief.

Sometimes bombs set off unlikely gestures of heroism. Chief Rabbi Israel Lau went on the radio in December 2001 to cite the bravery of an Arab man. Wounded in a Palestinian shooting rampage in northern Israel, he came to the aid of a young Jewish woman. Ripping off his shirt to make a tourniquet, he saved her life. Subsequently, the two lay in nearby hospital rooms.

Haifa is unique among Israeli cities: its mixed population of Arabs and Jews is vocal about the town's civic harmony. Yet Haifa's Arab population has not spared it from suicide bombers. When a 21-year-old bomber blew himself up on Bus16 as it traversed a biethnic Haifa neighborhood, Arab residents rushed to help Jewish victims who lay burned and bleeding upon the road. In the spring of 2002 the city was rocked by an explosion in a popular Arab restaurant. Among the diners were many Jews; they were fearful that a Jewish restaurant might be the target of a Palestinian attack, but they never dreamed they would be at risk in an Arab establishment.

This is not to say that many Arabs within Israel do not sympathize with the suicide attacks. Several Israeli Arabs have been arrested as aiders and abettors to Palestinian bombers. Mostly these Israeli Arabs helped by picking up a Palestinian who had sneaked over the border and then driving him to a location where he could then alight and cause his havoc. The cars driven by these Arab citizens of Israel have Israeli license plates, and so arouse no suspicion. Other local Arabs have been suspected as being behind the booby-trapping of cars that have exploded at preset times while parked in crowded Jewish neighborhoods.

When an explosion goes off, Arabs in the vicinity are in danger of mob violence. Either they may be snared as possible terrorists themselves or as people who aided terrorists, or they just may be the scapegoat for the frenzied vengeance of a crowd crazed by grief.

One such incident occurred in Netanya in March 2001, when a bomb exploded in mid-morning at the entrance to the popular open-air market teeming with shoppers. It was probably destined to be detonated within the market's crowded midst. But the bomber, upon seeing that he had been spotted, immediately exploded his bomb at the periphery, killing four and wounding sixty. Had he made it to his intended destination, the figures would have been much higher.

Within minutes of the explosion furious vendors formed a mob and cornered Salah Bassam, an Arab who had been working as a laborer for several years in the market. Dozens attacked Bassam and beat him nearly to death. Bassam spent two months in an Israeli hospital and upon release remained scarred and disabled.

The mob attack in the heart of Israel made the nation's news, but the lack of general outcry prompted outgoing Minister of Justice Yossi Beilin to advise his successor: "This ministry and its head must tell the people, with all due respect, 'Don't turn into wild animals.'"

Almost as terrifying as the primal rage that caused the attack on Bassam for a bomb he had nothing to do with was the fact that although many witnessed his assault, not one came forward to identify the attackers.

Opposition leader Yossi Sarid charged that the Netanya police did not want to conduct a serious investigation. Bassam reportedly knew some of his attackers personally, but refused to speak out. Netanya police claimed that they knew the identity of those involved but lacked evidence to bring charges. Finally some arrests were made, but no charges were ever brought.

Terror strikes indiscriminately, but it seems that most victims are the poor or the elderly, or young people in uniform. Many of the attacks take place on public transportation, used primarily by just these sectors of the population. It is usual even in traffic-choked cities for people who can afford it to get around via private car. As a matter of fact, two physicians killed in bus bombings were both using public transport while their own cars were being repaired. A Haifa man forced to sell his car because of financial difficulties took his only son for a day trip in March 2003; on their return home the bus they traveled on was blown up, and both died.

Another hard-hit sector is new immigrants from the former Soviet Union, who have swelled Israel's population by over a million in recent years. Upwardly mobile, industrious, and determined, many of these new immigrants are nevertheless still at the lower end of the economic scale, and thus just the ones to be taking the bus.

At 5:45 a.m. on May 18, 2003, the regulars boarded the first bus of the morning in the working-class Jerusalem neighborhood of Pisgat Ze'ev. When the casualties were tolled from the blast that rocked it, seven lay dead. Of them four were Russian immigrants: Marina Tsahivershivili from Soviet Georgia, who worked as a hospital kitchen worker; Nelly Perov from Kazakhstan, who held a cleaning job; Olga Brenner who worked at a Russian radio station; and 68-year-old Shimon Ostinsky. Ostinsky had been a lecturer in economics in Kiev, but in Israel he could not find employment in his profession, so he was on his way to his job as a parking lot attendant.

One of the most brutal attacks, which killed many young Russian Israelis, took place on Friday night June 1, 2001, not on a public bus, but outside a discotheque in Tel Aviv. Young people were lined up to get into the club and the bomber planted himself in the thickest place on line, then detonated his bomb. Twenty-one were killed, most of them young women. The reason for the female predominance was also rooted in economics: in order to attract more girls, the discotheque offered them free admission. Many took advantage of the offer, because for these Russian youngsters it was the only way they had of enjoying a night of dancing. Some parents of the deceased, who lived in other sections of the city, heard sounds of the blast and right away feared for their children's lives.

I was outside Israel the night of that bombing, and heard about it early the next morning on CNN in my hotel room in Barcelona. But

CNN just gave the general area, saying it was on the Tel Aviv seaside. Using an Israeli calling card to phone home, I was connected to an operator in Israel. Before giving her my number, I asked about the precise location of the attack. In such circumstances, one talks to strangers, even telephone operators on another continent. It was on the seashore, she told me, on the way toward Jaffa.

"You mean at the Dolphinarium?" I asked, using the common parlance for a spot that in the 1980s had housed an aquarium featuring live dolphin shows, and had subsequently been transformed into night spots. The name Dolphinarium had stuck.

"Yes," she answered darkly. "Where the Dolphinarium was—until last night."

For the next day and a half I wandered aimlessly around Barcelona, unable to enjoy its beauty, returning repeatedly to CNN in my hotel room. Some foreign airlines stopped flying to Israel that weekend because their crews spent their overnight stopovers in Israeli hotels near the Dolphinarium. Flight crews from Air France and Delta had heard the blast as the attack took place, and were stunned and fearful. Since the Dolphinarium bombing most foreign airlines have permanently changed their flight schedules to cut out the necessity of overnight layovers in Israel. Their crews fly in, refuel, pick up outgoing passengers, and take off again soon thereafter.

Another random victim was Adam Weinstein, a ninth grader killed in a Jerusalem bombing in December 2002; the media reported his age as "14 and a half." That "half" epitomized the tragedy. Adam died at an age where a half-year still matters. At his funeral, when Adam's older brother was asked his feelings about his brother's death, he murmured, "I wish it had been me instead of him."

And there are other victims, much less well known: Arabs themselves who fall victim to Palestinian terror. Arabs have been unwitting victims of bombs thrown by their compatriots, for when someone plans an indiscriminate killing, there is no knowing whom he may hit. I cut out of the newspaper the photo of a 1-year-old Arab baby lying in the hospital swathed in bandages beside her mother, her face covered with third-degree burns from the explosion on the bus she was riding in Hedera in the autumn of 2000. Shortly after another bombing at the entrance to a bus in Jerusalem in April 2002, which killed six and wounded ninety others, the injured Arab bus driver was interviewed on television from his hospital bed. Having helped the passengers on his bus escape the blast, his face and hands were badly burned, but he still had the heart to speak about his hopes for peace.

And in the January 2003 bombing in the old bus station section of Tel Aviv, home to many foreign workers both with legal working papers and without, twenty-three people were killed, including a Tel Aviv University law graduate. Five of the dead were foreign workers. More than a hundred were wounded, but many foreign workers were afraid to go to the hospital, and ran away to hide despite their injuries: they were apprehensive of being deported even from a hospital bed because their visas had run out. For the first and only time I remember, the television news made extraordinary broadcasts in English, giving the English-language hotline at the bottom of the screen, and assuring that nobody wounded that night would risk arrest or deportation. Shortly thereafter the minister of the interior took an exceptional step, giving a blanket extension to all foreign workers in Israel with expired visas.

A pregnant Israeli-Arab woman was also wounded in that attack. Her sister was soon to be married, and her husband had driven her and her two small children to Tel Aviv to buy her shoes for the wedding. She had just gotten out of her car when the bomb exploded, her body pierced by myriad shards of broken glass from the smashed windshield. The family was taken to a nearby hospital, where her two children were treated for shock. Doctors succeeded in saving her 6-month-old fetus.

Twenty-one-year-old George Elias Khoury was out jogging in his northern Jerusalem neighborhood on a March night in 2004. Khoury, the son of a prominent lawyer from an Arab-Christian family, was apparently mistaken by Palestinians for a Jew, and they gunned him down. Tragically, Khoury's grandfather had been killed in a 1975 terrorist attack in Jerusalem in which a bomb concealed in a refrigerator in Zion Square exploded. So Khoury's father lost both his father and then his son to terrorist attacks perpetrated by fellow Arabs in which they were mistaken victims.

Iman Tawil, a 13-year-old girl with leukemia in Jerusalem's Hadassah hospital, always had her father nearby. Rhalab Tawil had taken a job as a cleaner in the hospital to spend time with his daughter, often sleeping by her side. Since Iman was no longer hospitalized, Tawil spent the night of May 17, 2003, at his home in Shuafat north of Jerusalem. Early Sunday he boarded the first bus to work. He never arrived, because that was the targeted bus on which the four Russians died. Tawil, like his murderer, was a Palestinian himself.

The next day, when another 19-year-old Palestinian exploded her bomb at the entrance to a mall in Afula, death struck three persons. One was 41-year-old Hassan Ismail Tawatha. After fifteen years as an employee he dreamed of opening his own electronics business. Tawatha was not at the mall to shop. He was there as a student, attending a preparatory electronics course at a local college held inside. His entire village of Jisr a-Zarka turned up for the funeral. Tawatha, too, was an Arab.

And so the list goes, Arabs killed or wounded in attacks perpetrated by Palestinians who see themselves as heroes, and who are often perceived as martyrs in the communities from which they come.

What would their answer be if they knew their connection with these victims? Would they call it collateral damage, worthwhile for the cause they believe they are serving? What would Iman Tawil say to that, now that she has no father left? She and the other tertiary orphans?

Out of Israel's six million citizens approximately one million are Arab. Although the society is far from integrated, it is far from apartheid either. In Haifa Arabs and Jews live together in the same neighborhoods. On Jerusalem streets the two peoples rub shoulders daily, their children play in the same parks, and some attend the YMCA's binational kindergarten. In a northern town like Afula, or a southern one like Beersheba, Arabs and Jews ride beside each other on the escalators of the shopping mall.

When ambulances raced most of the seventy-one wounded in the Afula bombing blast to the Afula hospital, they were received by Dr. Aziz Daroushe, the Arab physician in charge of its emergency room. About 20 percent of the hospital staff and 40 percent of its patients are Arab.

Arab names regularly appear on the terror casualty lists. Shahada Dadis, the 30-year-old pharmaceutical representative shot to death in January 2002 while en route to Jenin with medical supplies; Maysoun Amin Hassan, the 19-year-old scheduled to study psychology at Haifa University, one of nine people killed in the bus suicide bombing in August 2002; Ahmed Salah Kara, the 20-year-old truck driver shot dead when a Palestinian gunman opened fire at an industrial depot in April 2003; Nizal Awassat, father of eleven, killed in August 2002 as he sat in a coffee house beside Jerusalem's Old City when a Palestinian terrorist opened indiscriminate fire; Suad Jaber, on her way to hand in the final semester paper for her degree in mathematics and statistics, among fourteen killed in a bus bombing in October 2002; 12-year-old Kamar Abu Hamed, killed with seventeen others on her way home from the eighth grade in March 2003.

The stories of Jewish victims are neither more nor less tragic. When people set out with murder in their hearts, there is no telling whose lives will be shattered. How can any be justified, how can any be glorified, how can any lead anywhere but to sorrow? These suicide bombers are not freedom fighters. They are guilty of murder aforethought.

Much has been written about the profile of the suicide bomber, what makes him do it, what kind of person he is likely to be. But one thing an observer of these bombings can be sure of: the bomber cares nothing about the identity of any of his victims. He would spare neither young nor sick nor old nor infirm. All are guilty in his eyes, or perhaps the guilt or innocence of the victims is irrelevant to his purpose, which is to kill the maximum number possible. In one bomb that went off in a religious Jewish neighborhood of Jerusalem, the bomber placed himself square in the midst of a group of young mothers waiting for their husbands outside a synagogue, all of them wheeling baby carriages.

And sometimes, there are unexpected victims. In the winter of 2001 a communal taxi carrying eight people was on its way from Tel Aviv up north to Tiberias. One of the passengers was a suicide bomber who sat quietly with who knows what plans. Then about an hour and a half out of Tel Aviv, on the Wadi Ara road, the taxi was stopped by a road-block. There had been alerts of possible terrorist infiltrators, and the police were checking every vehicle. The policeman approached the minibus, and all passengers were instructed to hand over their identi-fication papers. Just as his turn came and seeing he was about to be discovered, the bomber set off his explosive. The bomber did not die, but his left arm was blown off in the blast.

The one passenger killed was a 27-year-old recent immigrant from Chile named Claude Knafo. Knafo's traveling companion, Dafna, was wounded. Seven were injured in the blast, but just six were listed in the reports. Dafna was not among the names. That is because they list only people, and Dafna was a seeing-eye dog. Knafo, who was not blind, had been volunteering to act as the temporary owner of the 1-year-old golden retriever since she was a small puppy, raising her until she was old enough for the special training school seeing-eye dogs attend. The injured Dafna was found on the roadside next to the burned-out taxi. A local vet ad-ministered first aid on the scene; later, Dafna's crushed foot was oper-ated on, but her body remained riddled with shrapnel.

My husband has kept a Colt .38 Special locked in a drawer of our home in Israel for the past fifteen years. He has never fired it except in order to renew his gun license. I can count on the fingers of one hand the occasions it emerged from lock and key, to be taken with him on what he judges are potentially dangerous highways. Then he wraps the gun in an old felt shoe bag closed with a drawstring. Not exactly a Gunsmoke scenario.

I live far from the occupied territories, in a suburban town on the outskirts of Tel Aviv I like to think is sleepy and safe. I never touched this gun or any other until the Intifada, during a catered affair at a Jerusalem hotel.

Many guests stayed away that night, for travel to turbulent Jerusalem had become a calculated risk. In order not to insult the hosts, we chose to make the one-hour drive, but the gun went with us. The capital city had joined my husband's short list of hazards.

Once in the open, the gun becomes an albatross. Since it is illegal to leave a firearm unattended in an automobile, the gun had to come into the hall too. When my husband got up to fill his plate from the buffet, it fell to me to keep the pistol in my purse lodged between perfume and lipstick.

Close to midnight we got lost trying to find the highway back to Tel Aviv. Above all we were afraid of taking that infamous wrong turn leading straight to Palestinian Ramallah. Stopping at an intersection, we asked directions of the car beside us. "Straight ahead," its Arab driver said without hesitation. Continuing on the deserted road for a few minutes, we came upon a forbidding luminous sign "Barrier Ahead." Roadblocks? On the way to Tel Aviv? The suspicion that had passed through my mind seemed confirmed: the driver had deliberately misled us. A police van approached, its windshield guarded by a grill resembling the cage seen on nature shows when photographers venture into shark infested waters. But yes, the policeman corroborated, Tel Aviv was indeed straight ahead.

We had alighted on the new alternate highway winding through the occupied territories. Upon its completion, practical picturesque Highway 443 had become one of the heaviest traveled in the country. But not anymore.

As we drove those thirty minutes on that blackened road, I made small talk. My husband gripped the wheel with one hand and drove fast. He kept the other on the gun. We never saw another car until rejoining the main road in the center of the country. His gun rested unbeckoned.

On that same Highway 443 a 29-year-old driving instructor was fatally shot in the chest by assailants from a roadside ambush. Eliahu Cohen, new father of a 4-month-old son, was not killed in an armed robbery or because of a lover's quarrel. He was targeted by chance, for no other reason than he was of the wrong nationality in the wrong place. It could as well have been us, or anybody. Numerous deadly ambushes have been carried out on Highway 443; the perpetrators escape into adjacent Palestinian controlled areas under cover of night.

I am embarrassed to admit I have a firearm in my home; it contaminates our integrity. Guns are supposed to be for law enforcers, not for people like my husband who, as a cardiologist, is in the business of saving lives.

True, how significant is one quiescent pistol in the sea of violence that is the Middle East? Yet its lethal potential is a distorted fact of life that I cannot make my peace with. Nor can I in good faith oppose keeping it. Only when farsighted people in power finally dare to gamble on a larger peace will I feel able to insist we banish the ugly instrument.

Sometimes there are lulls, some for weeks at a time. They lure us into a false relaxation. And then the attacks start again, out of the blue, sometimes in clusters, often in expected places like Jerusalem or on public buses, at times way out in the periphery where nobody would dream it was unsafe to go. The list goes on and on: the Sbarro fast-food restaurant on Jaffa Street in Jerusalem demolished in August 2001, the poor people killed in an unlicensed pool hall in Rishon LeZion in the spring of 2002, the trendy young elite who took their coffee in the Moment Café in Jerusalem until it was blown up in the spring of 2002.

Attendees at a medical conference sponsored by New York University Downtown Hospital a few days before the second anniversary of the September 11 terrorist attacks heard Dr. David Applebaum, head of the emergency room at Jerusalem's Shaare Zedek hospital, deliver a talk about intake procedures and protocols at his hospital after terrorist attacks. Shaare Zedek has all too much experience in the field; by September 2003 it had treated over 550 wounded—40 percent of those wounded in Jerusalem since the start of the Intifada.

Applebaum, an American who had moved to Israel twenty years before, returned from the conference on the evening of September 9, 2003, a few hours before a new blast ripped apart Jerusalem's Café Hillel. Usually Dr. Applebaum was among the first doctors to arrive at the hospital after an attack, so his colleagues were puzzled, and then worried, not to see him. Dr. Applebaum had gone straight from the airport to Café Hillel to help celebrate his daughter's upcoming wedding scheduled for the next day. Both father and bride-to-be were among the seven dead.

Café Hillel, part of a chain, reopened its doors later that fall, as do so many of the targets. A few months afterward a friend who lives in Jerusalem suggested that we meet at another Café Hillel branch in the capital. At first I was too embarrassed to say I was reluctant to go where her life took her every day. But the out-of-the-way location I suggested proved inconvenient for her. Finally, I lay my cards on the table in an e-mail: "Michal, I hope your bravery in going to Café Hillel is contagious to me. I am not a Jerusalemite and I am also a coward. But when in Rome . . . so I will meet you at Café Hillel on Hillel Street. Hope you forgive my reservations." Michal's sardonic reply: "As the attack was at Café Hillel in Emek Refaim, I have neatly compartmentalized . . ."

The victims are such a stream that the dead are only news for one day. Soon they are remembered only by their own families, and new names take their place in the headlines.

I am no friend of the Israeli occupation, but I cannot see either how suicide bombers are a response to that injustice or how they will help bring it to an end. I have only known people like my husband who by lucky chance missed being where an attack took place, never anybody who was actually in one. But if I had, would I feel more conciliatory— or less so?

With every innocent Palestinian killed my heart sinks, not only at an individual's death, but because I feel morally implicated by the person who killed him—a Jew like I am—and because I know the circles of hatred against me and mine are widened by it. Random racial violence strikes Arabs as well—a young man stabbed in the back while doing nothing more provocative than walking into a mall. There are brutal anonymous murders on both sides, attacks that the radio calls of "nationalistically motivated," in current Israel newspeak.

Israelis vehemently oppose equating Palestinians killed by Israeli troops with the victims claimed by terrorist bombs. Their argument is that the army tries its best to avoid civilian casualties, but that inevitably they occur during the quelling of violent demonstrations or while targeting the terrorist leaders that Israel routinely hunts down and assassinates. But the line is not that clearly drawn.

In December 2002 an Israeli soldier shot at a Palestinian taxi that drove off in violation of a blocked road. The soldier's bullet struck someone in that taxi, and she died. The victim was a 95-year-old woman. Having lived so long, she might have remembered the Turkish soldiers before World War One, and she certainly remembered the long list of soldiers who followed. And then, at the end of this long life, to be killed by a soldier's bullet, who can stomach hearing of this travesty?

In February 2003 *Haaretz* ran this headline: "Gaza Woman, 65, Crushed to Death as IDF [Israel Defense Forces] Razes Stepson's Home." I read with nausea the details: the army carried out one of its routine ways of retaliating against people they identify as terrorists. It ordered everybody to leave the house, and then flattened it. Palestinian security officials claimed the stepmother of the suspect was partially deaf and apparently did not hear the warnings of the soldiers. Israeli military sources said that troops had scoured the house before demolishing it to make sure it was empty, but it began investigating the report.

These two incidents are but isolated examples. I do not know the details and the names of the many innocent Palestinian victims; they are reported in Israel only as statistics or as TV news footage of mass funerals. My heart goes out to them. But their deaths do not justify the taking of others.

As for suicide bombers, glorifying them seems obscene. Randa Ghazi's *Dream of Palestine*, a fictionalized account of a suicide bomber as hero, became a best-seller in France in the winter of 2003.

I wish its readers could also read about the everyday unglamorous people whose time on earth the bombers stole away, and about their families for whom the loss will never be filled. And even if they learned the story of but one victim out of the hundreds, they could not view the bombers as sacrificial heroes, but as individuals twisted into monstrosity.

One victim would suffice. The Ethiopian girl who lost her life on the way to the sixth grade. The volunteer doctor who never reached the hospital for crippled children. An anonymous manual laborer riding home bone tired from his hard day of work, thinking only of laying his head on the pillow and taking off his shoes. Or even, say, Claude Knafo, the gentle young man who brought up dogs to help the blind—the young man who, like so many other human beings in the Middle East, prematurely died a dog's death.

Chapter Seven *The Whole Country Is the Front*

My friend Rochelle and I first met at the women writers' peace conference in Tel Aviv in 1997, sitting near one another in a packed auditorium. In 1999 we found each other again on the Arab and Jewish Women's Walk for Peace along the recently opened Israel–Jordan border. The groups were distinct, but they danced in circles to each other's music, looked each other in the eyes, and traded smiles. That year—1999—was an optimistic time, when all the signs we could read pointed to better times yet to come. The last thing we foresaw was the outbreak of the Intifada a year later.

My professional and personal relationship with Rochelle was catalyzed on that march. From then on our frequent meetings have not been by chance. Yet as the times worsened, more and more of our communication was by e-mail and telephone.

Rochelle and I both live inside the original borders of the country set in 1948, but even though no military zones or occupied territories separate us, in the last few years the road between her house and mine has become an often treacherous course.

Rochelle, who moved from her native Canada to the Israeli countryside twenty-five years ago, found poetry in midlife, and more and more the world has been listening to her voice. Lines about the seascapes around her childhood Vancouver have given way to poems about the valleys and fields of her adopted home—and of the tragedies that abound in those beautiful vistas.

To drive the hour and a half to her home, I must wind my way through Wadi Ara, the main thoroughfare crisscrossing the country, lined with Arab towns and villages. In better times one traveled there without a second thought.

But since 2000 the Wadi Ara road has been spotted with blood. Buses have been repeated targets; in October 2002 fifty people were wounded and fourteen killed, including two Israeli-Arab victims, as 100 kilograms of explosives were detonated. At least one Jewish driver was shot dead point blank while stopped at an intersection.

A driver who missed the turnoff to Rochelle's small community would soon realize his mistake—road signs pointing straight ahead say "Jenin." In response to a particularly severe rash of bombings in the spring of 2002, Israeli tanks rolled into Palestinian cities that Israel had handed back to Palestinian control during the peace process. The Palestinians fought some of the most virulent battles in Jenin.

During the height of those battles, Rochelle's husband was diagnosed with heart disease necessitating urgent surgery. He was taken by ambulance to a Jerusalem hospital. Usually the patient's family must accompany the ambulance by separate vehicle, but the driver who had traveled the road filled with tanks and soldiers told Rochelle, "Missus, you better ride with us."

Jerusalem is too far for a daily drive back home, so Rochelle planned to stay in the city through her husband's recuperation. With Israeli violence constantly in the world's eyes, tourist hotels all over the country were closing or empty; Rochelle knew she would have no trouble making a reservation. But the hotel where she wished to stay was precisely the only one in town that was solidly booked. It was the guest house next to Hadassah University Medical Center—every single room overflowing with families of terror victims recovering from their wounds in the adjacent wards.

Rochelle lives not far from Mount Gilboa, where in 2001 a 17-year-old teenager was shot dead by a Palestinian sniper.

Not long ago farmers of the Gilboa region had big plans for expanded cooperation with Palestinians in nearby Jenin. Said Gilboa's mayor, "We paved that road four years ago and called it the 'economic path.' It was supposed to be the major thoroughfare for goods moving freely between communities in the Gilboa region and Jenin, in time of peace." That "economic path" has turned into a death trap for both sides. By the winter of 2003 desperate Gilboa farmers, fearful of more infiltrators, took matters into their own hands. They began to erect a separation fence adjacent to the road.

Spring brings to Mount Gilboa a rainbow of red and yellow wildflowers to rival any Monet canvas. It is home as well to a rare and wonderful species of black iris. Every March I want to make the journey to wander among those black irises. I go for the flowers—and to see my friend.

But how far things have descended since the day we first met: from the optimism of peace to the pessimism of avoidance. Spring brings irises, but never peace.

As the Intifada went from an incredible acute emergency to a way of life, lifestyles and mental attitudes underwent uncomfortable adjustments.

A young lawyer from Jerusalem with his arm in a plaster cast came to Tel Aviv. Wherever he went he was greeted with stares of sympathy followed by the identical question: "Were you hurt in an attack?" Shaking his head, he sheepishly related that his broken elbow had nothing to do with terrorism: he had tripped over his own feet walking down the stairs. People had been all too eager to assume his clumsiness had been heroism.

Although there have been attacks all over, certain locations have borne the brunt: Netanya, Kfar Saba, Hedera—all close to the Green Line. And above all, Jerusalem.

Jerusalemites themselves admit to skirting certain streets. Individuals have created private pockets of psychological safety. The rule of thumb seems to be: people feel safest in their own neighborhoods, no matter what objective reality might indicate. A man living in a kibbutz near the border with the Gaza Strip discovers that friends from the center of the country are too terrified to visit him. Yet he feels just the same when he leaves the safety of familiar surroundings. For him, walking the streets of Tel Aviv means feeling vulnerable.

Fewer shop in Mahane Yehuda, Jerusalem's open-air market, or Tel-Aviv's Shuk Hacarmel, whose large crowds and open stalls create a bomber's paradise. Some point to shoppers' folly in going there "just to save a few shekels." But for many with low incomes those few shekels multiplied by the week are still a substantial part of their budget.

Then there are those who insist on going to all their usual haunts, declaring, "I won't let terrorism change my life," as if showing prudence is in some way "giving in." And some believe that the violence is so random that precautions are irrelevant, and it's all a matter of luck, or destiny.

On the other hand, politicized individuals insist on traveling according to their convictions. Most glaring are the settlers on the West Bank and in the Gaza Strip; many feel their very presence upon the land is an ideological stand. The government of Israel gives them tangible support through subsidies and tax benefits. As heavily guarded as they are by Israeli soldiers, these settlers do indeed risk danger to live where they do, a risk they defiantly accept. Burning with the fire of conviction, and convinced of the rectitude of their mission, they are ready and willing to put their own lives and the lives of their small children on the line in the service of their beliefs. The land of Israel where they have settled, they insist, was given to the Jews by God in biblical times, and no modern political boundary is going to squeeze them out. In turn these settlers have lost many of their number to death at Palestinian hands.

One particularly horrifying incident happened in Gaza on May 2, 2004, when pregnant Tali Hatuel was gunned down with her four small daughters while driving, killed at point-blank range. One week later about 200 Jewish residents of Gaza went back to the site of the attack to hold a memorial service. During the service Palestinian gunmen began to shoot into the crowd of mourners, who took cover on the ground, and then were evacuated by the army. Since the army closed access roads when word came of the shooting, the father who had lost his wife and all his four children was unable to get through to the service in their memory. An army source commented that "in the Gaza Strip there are between three and ten shooting incidents every day in which the terrorists shoot at settlements, roads, and at IDF troops."

It could be argued that the settlers have accepted this risk, but also high has been the death toll among the young soldiers who are sent as part of their army service to guard these zealots. Some parents of these fallen soldiers hold the settlers as culpable for their children's deaths as the Palestinians who actually murdered them.

But for those who just want to live their lives without politicizing them, some places are too frightening to go to unless absolutely necessary. At the sight of the Jerusalem lawyer in a cast, those in the so-called safer zone seized the opportunity to demonstrate their solidarity. If they keep away from dangerous locations, they sympathize with those who live there. Mixed with their sympathy is an unspoken element of relief.

But then the wild-card element comes in. Safety is really nowhere. After a terrorist shooting spree in unlikely Beersheba, which left two young women soldiers dead, the mayor of Beersheba put it succinctly: "The whole country is the front."

Hardly anybody I know takes buses in Israel anymore, so I didn't feel a personal stab of fear one morning in January 2004 when my shaken husband phoned me from his car on the way to work: "A bus was just blown up in Jerusalem." But like thousands of others, I immediately turned on my radio, listening once again to the familiar litany: correspondents reporting above the wail of ambulances, interviews with trembling eyewitnesses, statements by spokesmen of one hospital after another on how many injured had arrived and the seriousness of their condition. Emergency phone numbers were broadcast over and over. One person died on the operating table at Hadassah hospital. Ten bodies were transported to the forensic institute for identification.

Nobody I knew, I thought, could be on that bus. Then I remembered Leora, the American law student in Israel for a year on a Fulbright grant. At my invitation just the day before, Leora had come by public transportation all the way to Tel Aviv University from her apartment in Jerusalem. Leora talked to my Israeli law students about the American experience of studying law, about taking the bar, about career choices and opportunities for international students. The Israelis asked question after question of their poised young contemporary. Until then, they had pieced together the American legal profession from television shows. Smiling, down-to-earth Leora brushed away the mystery, if not the glamour.

This morning, I thought, Leora might well be on a bus in Jerusalem. But when I telephoned her apartment there was an answer. Leora was shaken, but she was home. She was waiting until it would be almost dawn in the U.S. so she could call her parents and tell them she was OK before they heard about the bomb from somebody else.

And, it turned out, I had been wrong. Leora traveled only by private and communal taxis. "Not to ever take buses—that's one thing I promised my parents before coming here," she said. Since arriving, she followed security recommendations, keeping away from restaurants, markets, and crowded places. "Things had been so quiet here, that I was thinking maybe I should do more after all—until today," she said.

The attack wove its way into the day. At the post office, the radio was turned up so that all the clerks and customers couldn't help but hear. In the waiting room of a doctor's office the television broadcast live. The news split its coverage between the blast and the Israeli–Arab prisoner exchange which had been slated to monopolize the day's events.

A few hours after the blast, the street looked almost normal, the wreckage cleared, the blood washed away. Bus after bus again passed through the busy thoroughfare in the city's heart, packed with passengers. In the evening I tried to call Leora's apartment again. There was no answer. Along with others in the beleaguered city, she had gone out to play at living a normal life, until the next time.

Meeting with my friend and colleague Myla at the law school, she told me happily about her children's excellent elementary school in Haifa. But it had been a hard semester, Myla said. One of her daughter's third grade classmates had been killed at the start of the school year.

I learned that the third graders in Haifa's Reali School were used to the one empty desk in their Israeli classroom. At age 8, three months is an eternity, and the desk where Tomer Almog spent the first month of the term seemed like it has always been unfilled. After Tomer was killed with his grandparents, father, and seventeen others while having a family meal in Maxim's restaurant in Haifa on October 4, 2003, his school held memorials, psychologists visited his classmates, and for several weeks his photo and candles blanketed the desk. The boys in the class took it hardest, said Myla, because at that age they were closer to Tomer. Myla remembered Tomer's father from the second grade parents' meetings the year before.

In an instant, Tomer's mother became both widow and bereaved parent. But she lacked the luxury of grieving, for the explosion seriously burned Tomer's 4-year-old sister. It also immediately blinded one eye of his 10-year-old brother Oran and acutely injured the other eye. Specialists in the United States tried to save Oran from permanent blindness. After reconstructing the injured eye, the Helen Keller Eye Foundation for Research and Education head Dr. Robert Morris said that the best that could be hoped for was "walking around vision."

When the 29-year-old Palestinian woman, Hanadi Jaradat, calmly had lunch in the crowded restaurant before detonating the explosive belt hidden beneath her clothes, did she also know that the establishment she would decimate had been jointly owned and managed by Jews and Arabs for the past four decades? Her bomb killed five of her Arab brethren, mostly young people in their 20s and 30s, and injured the 90-year-old father of Maxim's Arab co-owner. Just days after the bomb, the management hung a banner across the wreckage: "We will not allow coexistence to be destroyed," and by December the restaurant had reopened its doors.

Then in January 2004 the bomber herself was reincarnated, prominently featured in an art exhibit in Stockholm coinciding with a conference on genocide. Entitled "Snow White and the Madness of Truth," her angelic face gazed from the sail of a miniature white boat floating in a large pool of liquid grotesquely dyed the crimson of fresh blood. An adjacent inscription postulated the death of her relatives and fiancé at the hands of Israeli forces as the motivation for Jaradat's act. The inscription seemed to indicate that understanding her act might justify it, while at the same time mourning her victims, including Tomer Almog's family. Ironically, it was not one of the commissioned Palestinian artists who created "Snow White" but rather an Israeli-born radical artist living in Sweden.

In an uncontrolled outburst during a reception, the outraged Israeli ambassador to Sweden, Zvi Mazel, angrily disconnected the installation's illumination and flung the wires into the bloodred pool. When with tremulous voice he tried to explain how he perceived "Snow White" as an indecent justification for murder, the ambassador was ejected from the hall.

The incident aroused ire in Sweden, including one reaction that if this is the way Israeli ambassadors behave, how much worse might be the conduct of their soldiers? The Israeli embassy in Stockholm,

renting the same premises since opening in 1954, was asked by the
landlord to relocate due to security concerns. The Israeli press and
media chewed every angle. The former Israeli ambassador to Sweden called Mazel's conduct counterproductive, suggesting that in
order to defuse anti-Israeli sentiment, he should have spoken to the
Europeans in their own language.

Each side rallied to its expected positions. The Israeli government
threatened to boycott the conference unless "Snow White" was with-
drawn. The Swedish ambassador in Israel responded that, although
perhaps in "bad taste," "Snow White" would stay. Jaradat's mother
insisted that her daughter was a martyr. The artist's aged mother, a
radical left winger living in an Israeli kibbutz, expressed pride in her son's
creation—and thereafter received anonymous death threats. Prime Minister Sharon gave a tired knee-jerk reaction, supporting Mazel's act as a
response to "mounting anti-Semitism."

As passions quieted, the museum removed publicity posters featuring close-ups of the bomber's face from twenty-six subway stations
around Stockholm, and after the Swedish foreign minister telephoned
her Israeli counterpart, Israel decided to attend the genocide conference.

For anybody who has been around unflappable silver-tongued diplomats, watching televised rebroadcasts of the Israeli ambassador's outburst
in Sweden was as startling as Khrushchev's banging his shoe upon the
table of the United Nations. But the furor around the ambassador's vandalism of a museum installation widened to embrace—and to symbolize—
the paradoxes and the ironies of the Israeli–Palestinian tragedy.

As usual, the ideologues used this undiplomatic diplomatic gaffe
and the brutal "Snow White" as grist for their respective mills. Meanwhile, Tomer Almog's desk remained empty, scar tissue formed over
his sister's burns, and his brother squints forever dimly at the world
through one reconstructed eye.

The furor over "Snow White" highlights another fallout of the
Intifada. While acknowledging that Israel is no saint, many in the
country feel it is portrayed in overly black tones by the foreign press,

especially in Europe. I have friends born in English-speaking countries who are adamant they no longer watch the BBC. Some blame Israel's PR instead of its deeds, maintaining that whereas the Palestinians have eloquent spokespeople like Saeb Erekat, the representatives of "our" side leave much to be desired. "If only we still had Abba Eban," they sigh, recalling the late Israeli diplomat who so brilliantly represented the country for decades. During the Six-Day War, when he spoke at the U.N. as Israel's foreign minister, my friends, family and I in New York hung onto his every word.

As the image of Israel deteriorated from a plucky vibrant democracy to that of a military oppressor of conquered people, and as Jewish institutions were frequently targeted around the world, Israelis asked the question: Is Israel's behavior—or perceived behavior—during the Intifada causing anti-Semitism? Or have the seeds of anti-Semitism been lying dormant and unexpressed, only to bloom again?

A British cartoon exemplified this phenomenon.

Ariel Sharon is immensely controversial, even in his own country. But is it legitimate to portray him as the inhuman devourer of Palestinian babies? Both the English newspaper *Independent* and the British press association apparently thought it was.

It began in January 2003, when the prestigious newspaper featured a cartoon by veteran caricaturist Dave Brown. A naked, debauched, and obese Ariel Sharon with grossly exaggerated Semitic features gobbles the body of a mutilated infant, clearly intended to be Palestinian. Clutched in his muscled grasp, the child's head has disappeared down Sharon's gullet, as Sharon's gaping jaws gnaw what is left of an arm. Sharon's private parts are covered by an election ribbon, while a tank advances over a ruined landscape and ominous helicopters swoop over the rubble of destroyed buildings repeatedly broadcasting the slogan: "Vote Sharon."

The cartoon was published a day before the 2003 Israeli election for prime minister, and came one day after the Israeli army had staged attacks on Gaza City. It also fell, whether coincidentally or not, on Britain's official commemoration of Holocaust Remembrance Day.

Brown's drawing depicted nothing less than a monster. And to any-body with even passing familiarity with history, the cartoon was a modern permutation of rabid Nazi anti-Semitic propaganda portray-als of Jewish vermin and the rebirth of the infamous "blood libel," which claims that Jews habitually slaughter Christian children. It is but a hop, skip, and jump from Dave Brown's demon Sharon to the propaganda posters of the Third Reich.

Brown defended his work as solely an election criticism of Sharon meant to encourage his rival, claiming it was neither anti-Semitic nor anti-Israeli and "sought only to target a man and a party I consider to be actively working against peace." But irrespective of Brown's pri-vate intention, after it was published the cartoon assumed a life of its own.

Among other protests, the Israeli Embassy in London lodged an official complaint with the British press complaints commission, call-ing the cartoon "anti-Semitic in a fantastically irresponsible way." The commission dismissed the complaint.

The clincher came almost eleven months after Brown's cartoon was published. On November 25, 2003, it was not only resurrected, it was crowned. The British Political Cartoon Society voted the cannibal Sharon from among thirty-four entries to be honored as the United Kingdom's "Cartoon of the Year 2003."

The Political Cartoon Society featured the cartoon on its Web site, and printing Brown's own defense against the charges of anti-Semitism, snidely requested, "Before any more of you get out of your pram about this cartoon, please have the decency to read below Dave Brown's ra-tionale behind the drawing."

Seeing the drawing resonating with the crude symbols of dark anti-Semitic tradition and demonizing a Jew as the cannibal of civilization, you didn't have to be Jewish to be outraged.

But Israel still generates passionate defense abroad from Jews and non-Jews alike. The most eloquent defense that came to my attention was the widely circulated article, "I Stand with Israel, I Stand with the

Jews," in December 2002 in *Corriere della Sera* by the celebrated Italian journalist Oriana Fallaci, long known for her leftist views. In paragraph after paragraph beginning with the words "I find it shameful," Fallaci accused Europeans of cloaking their anti-Semitism in sanctimonious condemnation of Israel: "I find it shameful . . . that state-run television stations [cry] only over Palestinian deaths while playing down Israeli deaths, glossing over them in unwilling tones. . . . I find it shameful that in obedience to the stupid, vile, dishonest, and for them extremely advantageous fashion of Political Correctness the usual opportunists—or better the usual parasites—exploit the word Peace."

As a member of the volunteer board of directors of the Fulbright educational exchange program in Israel until my term recently ended, my contacts with the brilliant students and scholars chosen to receive grants to the United States, and then hearing what they accomplish there, made me understand why this program can be viewed as one of the most significant American contributions to the world.

These are the things that went through my mind when I heard of the Palestinian attack October 15, 2003, in Gaza, which killed three American security personnel accompanying Fulbright committee members on their way to interview Palestinian Fulbright candidates and candidates for the related Humphrey program for professionals in public service. Those who planned the attack, pushed the detonator under the convoy, and later stoned American investigators, killed more than three individuals. They ironically targeted an American gift that works to their much-needed advantage.

The Fulbright program in Gaza is separate from the one in Israel, but it operates on the same principle, as do Fulbright programs worldwide: grants are provided for outstanding scholars to continue research and for students to pursue graduate studies in the United States—with the stipulation that they thereafter return to their countries of origin. American scholars and students, in turn, travel to institutions of higher learning around the world. The program is at once a brain exchange and an institutional ambassador for American civilization.

In the previous year nine students and three scholars from Gaza had traveled to the United States on Fulbright grants. An official at the American embassy felt that scholars who return to Gaza after the experience "have a new respect for the United States, and are able to see the nuances in our policies. They have come to love—they use this word—America." Fulbright applicants from Gaza in 2003 included students and scholars in the fields of psychology, mathematics, computers, medically related research, engineering, business, and public health—all desperately needed in that troubled society. But the wreckage of the bombed car—and the dead and wounded inside—traumatized the future of the Fulbright in Gaza.

Violence in Israel prompted many new measures to help ensure the safety of American Fulbrighters, ranging from intensive security briefings, an extra travel stipend to eliminate need for using public transportation, and guards at the program's offices. In the last few years, the Israeli Fulbright program maintained its vitality, with American students and scholars continuing to participate. No Fulbrighters left the country for security reasons, even after the devastating 2002 terrorist bomb on the campus of the Hebrew University in Jerusalem.

In Gaza, the picture is less rosy. Although American scholars did exercise their grants at Gazan universities during the 1990s, the U.S. Government travel ban imposed since the outbreak of the Intifada ended this arm of the program. Thus the Fulbright in Gaza is for the time being only a one-way street. Furthermore, its administration is disrupted by violence, including street battles, military closures, and roadblocks. Even after their scholarships have been approved, Gazan grantees often have difficulty crossing the border to the U.S. Embassy in Tel Aviv to apply for visas, and post-September 11 scrutiny delays the visa approval procedure.

But all that was nothing compared to what happened that October morning. After the attack all travel by American Fulbright officials into Gaza was terminated. Those Gazans slated to be interviewed on the day of the attack still had their chance—interviews were conducted by videoconferencing. American officials vowed that the Gaza Fulbright program will continue. But after this bloody obstacle, the future looks shaky at best.

The dearth of foreign tourists is widely bemoaned: ghostlike hotel lobbies, sparse airline flights, unemployed tourist guides. Yet in the next breath it is acknowledged: "Who can blame them for not coming?"

The same phrase can be repeated for Israelis reluctant to travel in parts of their own country. Who can blame them?

Israelis are inveterate voyagers abroad. For decades, the only way they could leave their borders was by ship or airplane. Americans can imagine the feeling by comparing it to someone living in New Jersey finding sealed before him the borders to Delaware, Pennsylvania, and New York. After the peace treaties, Egypt and Jordan opened up, but since the Intifada it is not safe for Israelis to set foot in either one.

Man may have walked on the moon, but Israelis have trod everywhere else. Estimates have it that just short of a million people travel outside the country every year for pleasure.

Hardly a one doesn't have his own personal story entitled, "The Most Remote Place in the World Where I Bumped into Another Israeli." Israelis encounter long-lost friends in the caves of Mesa Verde National Park in Colorado, at the underground mall in Canada's Edmonton, waiting on line at Disney World, and beside a tortoise in the Galapagos. There seem to be more Israelis in Katmandu than Sherpas.

"Stay seated until cable car comes to a complete halt!" cautions the notice in perfect Hebrew lettering atop a Swiss Alp. At a restaurant on the Burmese–Thai border 6,000 kilometers from Jerusalem, Israelis are right at home reading Hebrew tags identifying the buffet platters. Hebrew is heard on the handbag line at Bloomingdale's, on the escalator at the Louvre, at theater intermissions in London, on the Via Branco in Rio de Janeiro, on the train to Machu Picchu in Peru, and almost everywhere else.

And the problem is, nobody has to crane his neck to discern their language. Israelis are loud at home, and they remain loudly conspicuous abroad. They tend to congregate in big groups and expostulate in their native tongue.

Perhaps it is assumed that Israelis savvy enough to navigate the Amazon, master the New York City subway system, and tread their way through the back streets of Calcutta will be intelligent enough not to call undue attention to themselves. This is not the case. More than visible, they are positively hard to ignore.

"To whom do these suitcases belong? Who packed them? When? Where are you coming from? Did anyone give you packages to deliver?" Every air traveler leaving or returning to Israel is familiar with the questions seriously posed to frequent flyer and first-time traveler alike. Usually speaking in Hebrew helps cut short the security questions, but no one is exempt.

In February 2004, as I returned to Israel from a stay in New York, a young El Al security man decided to question me further. He insisted on my speaking English, asking me the names of all my relatives in Israel, and where my daughter went to school, and whether she would eventually plan to go to the army. "Where did I learn Hebrew?" he wanted to know. Then he persisted, asking what Jewish holiday was coming up.

"Purim," I answered.

"And what do we do on Purim?"

"On Purim?" I replied. "On Purim we celebrate the escape of the Jewish people from annihilation."

At that, the security man put all the little colored stickers on my luggage and motioned for me to pass on through.

Plane security may be tight, but what about security precautions to protect the Israeli roaming the length and breadth of the globe? I could find neither protocols, publications, guidelines, checklists, pamphlets, nor regulations. No travel agent gives out any brochure or advice. No airport security officer advises the traveler to keep guard on his person as well as his belongings abroad. Only youth delegations are advised to remove Hebrew baggage tags, refrain from wearing clothing with Hebrew writing, and not openly carry Hebrew guidebooks. To ferret out any recommendations at all, an extremely enterprising citizen can reach the obscure government Bureau for Counterterrorism where a courteous, underworked public official goes over prudent behavior and lists the countries to which the State of Israel discourages travel: all Arab countries and all Muslim countries except Turkey and Bali.

Israeli diplomats have been targeted over the years in diverse countries. But even private Israelis who felt prudence to be the better part of wisdom while at home exhibit little inhibition about standing out like a sore thumb once abroad.

El Al's vaunted security became in high demand after September 11. And European capitals have for years stationed armed personnel near flights departing for Tel Aviv. It is a sober reminder for the returning traveler that once he lines up for Israel he instantly becomes a potential target. In just this way, two persons met their death in Los Angeles in June 2002, when an Arab attacked the El Al counter processing passengers for a flight.

Flying from Israel to Europe, I have seen armored tanks standing ready on the runway to escort the arriving plane, a bittersweet reception committee. And when Israel-bound, I have been directed to special terminals, had my flight numbers go unmentioned on departure boards, have left from unmarked gates, have had my hand luggage combed over, and had to identify my suitcases on the runway. As elated as one may be from the most wonderful trip abroad, this special welcome can sink anyone's spirits. Relaxation may have started to feel like second nature abroad. The pressure cooker begins bubbling even before the beleaguered strip of Israeli sand and the hazy skyline of Tel Aviv become visible through the airplane window.

"I never promised you a rose garden." These were the words superimposed on a photograph of a dried and prickly thistle in an Israeli government poster once aimed at encouraging idealistic immigration from the West. In New York City I had that poster taped to my wall.

It was axiomatic that choosing life in Israel entailed material sacrifice, the unstated corollary being that it offered spiritual enrichment. Whether that corollary will be borne out is a sadly decreasing possibility. The irony was that by the time I arrived true idealism was on its way out, and in its stead materialism ensconced upon the pedestal where it now reigns without challenge.

But when we arrived the part about material hardship was resoundingly true.

Israeli institutions were created from scratch and precedents made up as they went along. Hundreds of thousands of poor immigrants were absorbed, and a country with few natural resources struggled to make itself viable as well as independent. Furthermore, the early state espoused the principles of its socialist roots, which expressed themselves in extensive social legislation, and an economic and taxation system full of controls.

For example, a restrictive trade policy imposed prohibitive taxes on imported goods, and things a person like me had always taken for granted as necessities were either unavailable or exorbitant. Minor conveniences that seemed in the United States to be too inconsequential to mention became sorely missed once they were absent.

So in the old days sailors used to set up folding tables on Tel Aviv streets to hawk Lux soap and Gillette razors. When my family shipped our household furnishings from the U.S. in a container, we bought cases of Pampers and stuffed the empty bookshelves with as many disposable diapers as they would hold. Two boxes of Pampers were considered a nice baby gift for a newborn, to be kept aside for special outings. Canned baby food was sold by pharmacies one jar at a time. Rough tissues came in a big roll, which had to be cut with scissors into individual pieces. Freezers, clothes dryers, food processors, fountain pens, blue jeans, sneakers, and, above all, automobiles bore astronomical price tags.

In a climate approximating Florida or Texas, air conditioners were no exception. Families saved up for a single unit, installed it in one room, and all gathered there to cool off. In the cold stone houses during winter, heaters were turned on with Spartan frugality to minimize high costs of electricity or fuel.

But there was one facet of life American immigrants felt smug about, and routinely trotted out as an example to minimize the difficulties.

In Israel, they said, the streets were safe.

There were always wars, of course. Traffic fatalities were high. But if burglaries were not infrequent, one never feared that the intruders might shoot, or even be armed. And violent street crime, which plagued American streets, was virtually nonexistent.

The Intifada put an end to that boast.

Now people walk glancing over their shoulder, eyeing the coming pedestrians with suspicion, and unwillingly becoming adept at "street smarts." None of these techniques is particularly effective against an Intifada.

"Where I live is safer than Lake Wobegon!" That's what I used to tell friends from abroad who were jittery about visiting a place like Israel. "In my town you can walk down the street alone at 3 a.m. and not worry who may be walking behind you," I would say. "People lock their doors against burglars, not murderers or arsonists."

Less than a month into the Intifada, I could not say it anymore.

From my top-floor window, I love to glimpse a thin strip of the Mediterranean Sea half a mile away. And rising from a seaside cliff, I see the minaret of an old Arab mosque called Sidnei Ali. It is still in use. On Fridays, buses from all over Israel pull up, filled with Moslems who attend prayers there.

One limpid evening in early October 2000 my friend Francoise heard commotion outside. Thinking it was one of those big beach parties again, she went out on the roof balcony of her Herzliya home near the sea. But instead of music Francoise heard the chants she never thought would be uttered in her neighborhood: "Death to Arabs!"

Two hundred fifty Jewish demonstrators, incensed by the nascent Palestinian uprising, were charging up to Sidnei Ali. A grenade landed on the mosque's balcony, but caused no damage. When the mayor of Herzliya arrived on the scene after midnight to plead with the mob, they shouted invectives at her. Police discovered a barrel of gasoline; the caretaker's son noticed a crate of grenades. Police arrived in force, keeping the mob away from the mosque. Arrests were made, and finally the rabble dispersed. For the next few days policemen and soldiers were posted beside its doors.

I had passed by Sidnei Ali countless times on my way down to the most beautiful beach in Herzliya. The previous winter my daughter and I had taken sketchbooks and pastels to draw the graceful mosque, the palm trees surrounding it, and the worshipers on their way inside.

I had driven by on my way to visit the nearby archaeological site of Apollonia, the ruins of an ancient city founded by the Phoenicians, named by the Greeks for their god Apollo, and then settled successively by the Romans, Byzantine Arabs, and Crusaders.

The day after the riots, I passed through the doors of the mosque for the first time. The imam—the Moslem priest—had only words of praise for the police protection and the mayor.

"We have to keep talking," the imam said. "We cannot throw away the threads of friendship that have been sewn."

The demonstrators were thought to have come from poorer neighborhoods on the other side of town, for the mosque sits near an affluent area, close by the residence of the American ambassador and other diplomats.

While I was there a steady stream of Israeli Jews from the neighborhood came by to convey their solidarity. They stopped as well by a long-time Arab restaurant on the highway in Herzliya, and not because they were hungry. They came only to drink a tiny cup of sweet dark coffee—and to shake the owner's hand. The restaurant was open for business, as it has remained throughout the Intifada years that have since passed. But in a combination of fear and hostility, many Jews now stay away from Arab establishments, and its business never approaches the full house it used to see before.

But that week another Arab restaurant in town was shut, a heavy green tarpaulin covering its doors where a photo of the slain Yitzhak Rabin had been displayed for years. On the same night the mosque was attacked, unknown arsonists, perhaps part of the mob that had later stormed the mosque, burned down its storage warehouse and the adjacent rented house where the Arab owners lived. The house was empty, because due to the tensions the owners had fearfully stayed in their home village near Tiberias. A heavy smell of smoke hung over the corner where the buildings stood; crates of new green lemons that escaped the fire waited for tahini to again be prepared.

The charred restaurant was down the road from the school where my elder daughters had gone to high school, around the corner from the pool where my youngest daughter goes daily to swim practice, and beside the gas station where I often fill up my tank.

It felt like the country was a ship springing a thousand leaks at once. And one of those leaks, albeit minor, had been near us. The Intifada was not just a headline in the paper. It had early come close to home— although in Herzliya it was violence in reverse: attempts against the tiny population of Arab merchants.

To its credit, the town moved swiftly to cool tempers of frustrated youth, the element most prone to violence. It quickly set up programs in schools and community centers to diffuse the tension.

The dunes outside the mosque at Sidnei Ali are a place where lovers usually go to park. No lovers came that October week. Nobody I knew shared the hatred that targeted Sidnei Ali, but all were overwhelmed with the dread that, along with Jewish and Arab holy places, a serenity that was almost in our grasp had been trampled.

Time bore us out. Serenity became obsolete. Even though hardly any violence has revisited my area, I have never since dared describe my town as Lake Wobegon.

The sixth of October, which fell a week after the Intifada erupted, is a date burned into the historical consciousness of both Israelis and Arabs, remembered either with sorrow or with pride. For Israelis, it marks the biggest military shock ever suffered: a surprise attack by Egypt in the midst of Yom Kippur, the Jewish Day of Atonement, in 1973, catching the whole nation in a shameful strategic slumber. For Egypt, despite the ambiguous outcome of the conflict, the date has remained a proud symbol of avenged national honor. A central plaza in Cairo is Sixth of October Liberation Square, and innumerable Egyptian restaurants and streets bear that name.

October 6, 2000 saw Palestinian riots erupt in Jerusalem near the Temple Mount after Friday prayers. Youths hurled stones at Jewish worshipers at the Western Wall, and the Palestinian and Hamas flags were briefly hoisted over the Temple Mount. An Israeli police station beside the Lion's Gate to the Old City was trashed and burned, and police rescued eight injured policemen trapped inside. Ten Palestinians died that day across the land in what Palestinian leaders termed a "day of rage." So ended the Intifada's first week: blood bringing more blood, the domino theory of hatred.

Nineteen years before, on October 6, 1981, Egyptian President Anwar Sadat, pioneer of rapprochement with Israel, was assassinated by Islamic fanatics. The day of Sadat's assassination my family and I were due to leave for a camping trip beside the Red Sea in the Sinai Desert. Sadat's murder turned the region into temporary turmoil, raising questions of security. Still, we chose to drive down anyway, and spent the following nights under peaceful desert stars.

By coincidence, on October 6, 2000, we were again set to drive down to the Sinai. The fall is the best season beside the Red Sea, and we had been holding reservations at an Egyptian bungalow resort since May. But unlike 1981, we canceled this trip without a second's hesitation. So did everyone we knew. Even the adventurous stayed close to home. Roads throughout the country were closed. Rocks were hurled by Arabs at Jewish vehicles. The stench of burning tires filled the country's air.

During those early Intifada days my friend Diane from Boston sent me an e-mail of support: "Sometimes from afar it is worse than when one is there, on the spot," she wrote, then went on perceptively, "This time it seems as if everything is just as bad as we imagine."

So, my family did not go snorkeling in the Red Sea. On that weekend I lost my vacation. Others lost their lives.

It was just the very beginning, and we were still sure the hurricane would pass. For months we listened eagerly to every new peace initiative, believing that everybody would soon return to their senses, and if they didn't do it on their own, President Clinton would make sure they came around. But as weeks passed and then months, the abnormality of normal existence became the status quo of Israeli life. People stopped holding their breaths at every mini-summit. Acute trauma turned into chronic illness. As time brought an increase instead of a diminution of death, life turned into a roller coaster ride where every day brought another precipitous plunge. The deviant became the norm, and catastrophe the routine.

The meteorologist on duty delivers the daily weather forecast on morning radio. Ending as always with wishes for a good day, one began to inject, almost as an afterthought, "Just let it be a quiet one." Every listener in Israel knew he wasn't referring to the wind.

From conferences to school outings, from family picnics to work-related trips, "the Situation" has become a variable always to be factored in. The short phrase says it all—a shorthand catchword understood nationwide. Finally it even infiltrated the weather forecast.

If there has always been the Situation, it has never seemed so omnipresent. It shadows everyone, no matter where they fall on the continuum from extreme right to far left. If settlers continue to live in the occupied territories out of an ideological conviction aided by government subsidy, other Israelis must travel there to provide the settlers with services. Telephone technicians and fuel suppliers, for example, regularly cross the Green Line to sort out problems and make deliveries. Although they travel in vans with reinforced windshields and accompanied by armed guards, it's not an assignment they look forward to.

The economy is stricken. But two sectors are ironically booming. One is the personal protection industry, reporting a 100 percent increase in sales of canned tear gas and pepper-spray cans. Huge sums are spent on armored school buses to drive the children of settlers to school. Cell phone companies aim advertisements at the settler population, claiming that having a cell phone will aid in their security, as in one pointed slogan: "With Pelephone you are never alone."

As foreign investment in the Israeli economy plummets and firms go out of business, jobs as personal security guards are plentiful. An armed guard is now required by law to be posted outside restaurants and cafés. To offset the cost, a "security surcharge" is added to many bills. These security guards, many of them young people after army service supplementing their income as they prepare for or attend university, are the ones who often discern the lethal danger coming. So, for example, the guard who died after accosting the bomber at a commuter train station in Kfar Saba in late April 2003. The guard who detained a bomber the following week at a pub in Tel Aviv was seriously wounded. The guards put their lives on the line, and by stopping the bomber before he proceeds deeper into the crowd, minimizes the carnage and saves others. Whereas the Palestinians glorify their suicide bombers, the closest to Israeli heroes are the guards who die while preventing attacks.

Another industry quietly doing well is the moving business. Some foreign corporation employees pulled out early in the Intifada. Foreign companies and embassies often aim to send personnel without dependents, and since the Intifada began, enrollment at the American International School fell by one third.

Unknown numbers of Israelis leave too, prompted by a mix of economic woes and psychic stress. In the spring of 2001 an individual charged with financial improprieties skipped the country. When reporters caught up with him in New Jersey he vehemently denied having left to escape his creditors. Instead, he tried to pin it on the Situation: "We left because it was too dangerous for the children."

Taxi drivers were exposed a few years back as bilking tourists. Now this gruff, no-nonsense group has become the country's welcoming committee. With foreign visitors few and far between, taxi drivers offer a spontaneous and genuine "Thank you for coming" accompanying every ride.

When I heard writer Susan Sontag accept the 2001 Jerusalem Prize, the prestigious literary award highlighting a writer's social contributions, I was not surprised that neither she nor Ehud Olmert, the right-wing mayor of Jerusalem, could resist injecting into their speeches their respective take on the Situation.

If everything is under this black shadow, it looms larger when people try to ignore it. There is a surreal aura to loud parties, or the attempt to carry on as usual. Personal issues and disappointments, and other pressing social problems, take a back seat to the black fog. It feels obscene to leave the Situation out of sight for long. People seem perplexed, at a loss for strategies, without a tether. If a few quiet weeks go by, they say with hope that the Situation seems to be getting better. But the quiet never lasts for long, for the Situation is not an intermittent troublesome risk. Instead, it has become a debilitating disability, a gash on Israel's Achilles heel, bleeding anew with every footstep.

One of our friends' 20-something sons regaled us one evening with Situation jokes so gory and offensive they made us cringe. But black humor and bad taste may give young people a psychological handle on the uncontrollable.

The abnormality of normal life has become the status quo. The best thing about going to a movie or the beach or a wedding is that you can't listen to the news. Buying popcorn at the movie, spreading out a towel and putting up an umbrella at the beach, and bumping into old friends, watching the ceremony, and dancing to upbeat music at a wedding—these mundane activities make normalcy return for a few hours.

But a short interlude is not enough to really unknot the coils. Coming back to one's car or one's kitchen, fingers reach for the radio knob. The temporarily suspended compulsion returns: to hear what's happened. Almost always something has. Having gotten a fix of the latest jarring headlines, one can switch off until the fix wears off in time for the evening news, the late-night recap, or the early morning briefing.

To live in Israel today is to live with a permanent disability of the nerves. The nation's daily schedule is punctuated by a self-inflicted compulsion to hear the worst as soon as it happens.

Some people keep an ear cocked for the news all day, some have imposed a sanity-saving regime of listening only in the morning and at night, some have stopped looking at the media altogether. But the news is written on people's faces as well, in their tense body movements, in their hesitation to make long-term plans, even in their frenetic hedonism.

Loud noises make people jump, and jump to conclusions. Attending the festive end-of-year Fulbright Foundation dinner in 2001 for the scholarship grantees on the beautiful lawn of the American ambassador's residence, the noise of air force helicopters suddenly droned overhead, flying northward along the coast. For the quarter of an hour the noise lasted, an unspoken nervous mood pervaded, with me and other guests looking furtively up at the sky, wondering if we were watching the start of some new military operation.

Every explosion reverberates through the country. Strangers stop each other on the streets. Within minutes, everybody seems to have heard. If surroundings look the slightest bit out of the ordinary, we jump to the conclusion that "something has happened."

Once, noticing the driver in an adjacent car shaking her head from side to side and staring at her radio, I understood I had better turn mine on. I wasn't wrong.

Explosions have become part of the landscape. "How many dead?" children blurt out when told of an attack. Callous? No. They are only mouthing what the rest of us are thinking.

The media has greedily stepped in to the fray. Even before ambulances arrive, reporters are there, materializing out of nowhere to cover the gruesome stories. They switch back and forth from the scene of the attack to entrances of hospital emergency rooms, to spot interviews with eyewitnesses, mayors, rescue workers, and people frantically looking for relatives.

We have become catastrophe freaks, hungry for sensational facts: that a burned 6-month-old baby wore a clown suit, that one of the dead was a social worker who herself had helped comfort families of previous attacks. Shortly after one bombing, I saw a TV reporter point his microphone at an injured man lying in a hospital bed and broadcast a live interview minutes before the man was wheeled into surgery. The front pages of the mass dailies publish color photos of rivulets of blood and the faces of anguish on the wounded. Nevertheless, there is across-the-board self-censorship of the most gruesome pictures, and the names of the dead are not released until families have been notified.

Concomitantly, those injured in prior attacks soon leave the limelight, left alone to contend with their wounds, their rehabilitation, their disabilities, and their reduced lives.

As the one-year anniversary of the lethal Passover 2002 bombing in a Netanya hotel approached, a television program featured an update on five women wounded in the attack. They emerged from obscurity onto the screen with open physical and psychic wounds. It was an unusual revisit to a few of the 544 Israeli civilians severely injured, 779 moderately injured, and 4,103 lightly injured, statistics released by the Israel Ministry of Foreign Affairs as of April 1, 2004.

Four of the women had been trying to earn extra money by working as waitresses that night. Three were originally from Russia, and one was a Moroccan Moslem. The fifth woman was an Israeli whose husband had taken the family out for Passover seder to the hotel. "Why should you have to cook?" he had said to his wife. He was killed outright in the blast, and the woman's 19-year-old daughter suffered a head wound leaving her blind in one eye, and with permanent brain damage. A year later, the young woman is still relearning how to speak. The impassive stone-faced mother was pictured encouraging her daughter on the air: "Before you were a beautiful Shiri with two eyes, now you are a beautiful Shiri with one."

One young Russian woman was a dancer moonlighting as a waitress. Now confined to a wheelchair, she described strangers' stares as she maneuvers her way in public. Another Russian, a dark-haired beauty who had been a math teacher by day and a part-time waitress by night, now hardly ever leaves her apartment. The Moroccan woman, still living in the Park Hotel where the blast occurred, sought her out and visited her regularly. The two from opposite worlds have become friends, a camaraderie born of misfortune. The Moroccan was still undergoing physiotherapy, her right hand paralyzed. Hotel staff volunteered to come in daily and help her dress.

The last, a middle-aged Russian woman, has continued to work as a waitress at the same hotel. "What can I do?" she asked. "I have to earn a living."

All five were apprehensive as the anniversary date approached. Passover would never again be a holiday for them.

The report was a shock to Israeli viewers, who have somehow put out of mind the inevitable follow-up to terror. Some have made it their business to volunteer in rehabilitation hospitals, or take the families of victims under their wing. But most plunge headlong into the future, trying not to be dragged down by the tragedy of others.

Immersed in gore, it is no wonder that general sensitivity and sensibility decrease. How can a single case of spousal homicide, a worker blinded because of faulty work conditions, or a child run over by a school bus have the impact they normally would or be prompts toward social action? People have desensitized themselves to violence as a defense mechanism. Consequently, they are less moved by violence close to home among their own, and all the more so regarding violence and human rights abuses upon those of the other side.

Israelis feel they need to go abroad to take a break. First and foremost the traveler is struck by tremendous relief. Just to be away, in quiet, in the absence of ominous updates, is worth the price of any ticket. The Eiffel Tower, the Aegean Sea, the Scottish moors are all secondary. What counts is to be *out*.

Arriving from Israel into another society, I have been shocked to see people pursuing their lives with little to worry about except themselves. At first glance it seems superficial, self-indulgent, and trivial: going through the day encapsulated in private existence.

But if the lack of generalized tension initially appears like a void, the realization strikes that perhaps it is the bombarded Israeli who lives in a personal void. Because in Israel now a person is not just himself. He is himself plus the Situation, a condition no easier to shrug off than a hunchback.

The Situation is the unwanted Siamese twin, the boil about to explode, the itch that torments, the growth you hope against hope is just benign. It pushes personal issues aside.

When you are terrified of a bomb, or a bullet, or a war, you don't have to confront yourself. You don't have to decide if you've chosen a life of meaning. Personal issues are not only preempted by the Situation, the Situation is a good excuse to avoid facing them. But if time abroad lengthens, the important questions of self that have been brushed aside rush back. Suddenly abroad a person sheds that unwanted yet strangely insulating disability. No hunchback, no boil, no tumor. He may be forced to ask, "Who am I?"

The cauldron robbing people of their inner complexity has no boundaries. Focused on crises and developing a morbid fascination with public events they feel powerless to affect, their edges have been smoothed and their personalities less distinct. Masochistic obsession with daily calamities, although understandable, carries a price. The lack of psychic leisure has turned personal introspection into another casualty figure. The sardonic truth is that Israel is a place where it is impossible to relax.

The occupation has hardened Israelis to injustice, and not just toward Palestinians. When the 23-year-old American peace activist Rachel Corrie was run over and killed by an Israeli bulldozer in the spring of 2003 while she stood on the heap of dirt to protest a house demolition in Gaza, no general outcry was heard in Israel. The story did make the news, there were some protests and reports, but the society did not stop cold in its tracks or rise up in a shout of outrage. Perhaps people thought the army would honestly investigate, perhaps they felt that Corrie was more an instigator than an innocent, perhaps they could not be shocked at one more death in death-soaked Gaza. This indifference would not, I think, have taken place in the days of Rabin, Begin, or Ben Gurion.

Within the de facto state of the "Greater Israel," Jews are no longer the underdog. If in fact they recall when they were, they do their best to push it deep into their subconscious. They miss the point that strength alone cannot mean survival. Because when they forget the righteousness and the concern for justice embodied in their heritage they themselves create lethal fissures in the raison d'être of nationhood.

One Israeli friend of mine did act that way, a small unpublicized and unchronicled act of courage and heroism, which she herself performed unconsciously, and even against her better judgment.

It happened around Independence Day a few years before the Intifada, but during a time when suicide bombers were blowing up buses with sickening, if unpredictable, regularity.

Patriotism, like almost everything else in Israel, is far from subtle. Every spring beginning several weeks before Independence Day, blue and white plastic streamers, the national colors, wave from street lights and telephone wires in every Israeli town, and polyester flags overflow the sales bins beside supermarket checkout counters.

The great majority of drivers whizzing down the highways clip miniature flags onto car windows, blatantly flourishing their loyalty. With the roads a blur of blue and white, there seems to be no space left for ambiguity.

My friend displays no flag, but she is nonetheless a patriot for not wearing her heart on her sleeve. Patriot, or traitor, she isn't sure what to call herself. But I am.

Not long before Independence Day, she stood at the window of her apartment in the suburb of Herzliya gazing at a winding patch of secondary road below. As usual, Palestinian laborers from Gaza and the West Bank were congregating at the informal pickup point beside the road, where Israeli contractors came daily to fill their labor needs with one-day migrants. By afternoon, the Palestinians would be back on the bus that sped them out of Israel proper before dusk.

As she gazed down, she saw a police van pulling off the road and stopping next to the group of Arabs. It was not labor law violations the police had at the back of their mind in these routine spot checks. Any man without proper entry papers was immediately high up on the suspect list as a potential terrorist.

All at once she noticed two figures detach themselves from the group and bound away, running crouched over through the adjacent fields. From her vantage point a few stories up, she could discern that they were not much more than boys in their teens, their thin bodies running with the panic of fleeing deer.

She saw them turn this way and that, hunting for a place to hide. Just as the police van loomed close, they ducked behind the brambly bushes of a thistle plant. They became one with the ground, only their eyes stared wide. Because the pair were concealing themselves, they clearly had no papers. It was obvious they were infiltrators. True, they were teens, but teenagers are often the most dangerous.

"Terrorists!" my friend thought, panicked. "Who knows, their pockets might even now contain grenades ready for detonation, butcher knives, stolen revolvers . . ."

Getting out of the van, the two policemen sauntered over to the cluster of Arabs still standing by the roadside. Each man fished in his pockets and obediently held out his documents for inspection. There was no reason for the police to suspect that two others were concealing themselves in the nearby bushes.

She snatched the telephone receiver and dialed police emergency. She had to turn them in.

But before the police station answered, she hung up.

She stared at the two human beings crouching in the dirt. In her mind passed footage of the innumerable hunted, oppressed, and fugitive throughout the ages, at the perpetual mercy of the powers-that-be. This woman—Israeli-born, generations removed from pogroms, and personally far from the genocide of World War Two—saw before her not the semi-arid Middle East, but a fleeing pair in a snowy forest running for their lives from their fascist pursuers.

She couldn't bring herself to make the call. She watched as the police, finding all in order, drove away. After fifteen minutes, the two boys rose out of the thistles and trod warily back to the group. In a second, they became indistinguishable from their comrades.

All day she waited to hear the news of the attack launched by the men whose escape she had abetted. She thought of her own son and daughter—both soldiers, both out there riding buses every day in their olive-colored uniforms. Sitting targets. She knew as well as the next person that the pair she had let go free might be the suicide bombers who would board the very bus her child was riding.

Her decision wasn't prudent, or logical, or even conscious. But without knowing it, she had weighed two principles, and had chosen faith in humanity. For she, too, believes that people are really good at heart. She had looked down at those scared boys, and wanted them to be benign, knowing full well they might nevertheless be filled with hatred and anger and political sentiments she would find abhorrent.

But she refused to assume them to be murderers. Instead, she acted on the conviction that they were so desperate for work that they were willing to take the risks of sneaking in without papers, and of exposing themselves to arrest, to administrative detention without trial, or to worse.

There was no terror attack that day. And maybe the boys did manage to pick up a few hours' wages at a building site.

Detestable political realities force us all into untenable moral dilemmas. Independence Day in Israel comes on the heels of Passover, when we are told, "Remember when we were slaves in Egypt." Some of us do.

The State of Israel was founded as a great utopian experiment. That it was born at all was a true miracle, but Israel means nothing if it doesn't remember its past—not in order to justify its own existence, but to behave with empathy toward those who are weak today, and especially the weak whom Israelis themselves rule over. The challenge of the Jews in a Jewish state is to be worthy of their own history.

Chapter Nine *Daring Yet to Dream*

The great mass of Israelis may have lost faith that the peace movement can hold out a lifeline. But a minority dedicated to coexistence continues to plug on, flying in the face of the odds, of safety, and at times even of the law.

American born, raised, and educated Rabbi Arik W. Ascherman is the prototype of radical clergy throughout history who have broken away from the mainstream to march at the vanguard of social protest. Bearded Ascherman looks like a modern-day prophet. A reform rabbi, he heads Rabbis for Human Rights (RHR), which comprises rabbis of all Jewish streams. His civil disobedience has included physically blocking Israeli bulldozers about to demolish Palestinian houses built in violation of building or zoning ordinances, leading to his arrest and criminal indictment.

Rabbis for Human Rights has its office on Jerusalem's Asa Street near the site where several bombs have exploded. From there Ascherman and his supporters regularly travel to the territories to help with Palestinian planting—to offer extra hands, to make a statement of solidarity, and in the hope that Israeli witnesses will lessen chances of violence.

In addition, Ascherman and RHR have put themselves on the line against the route of the so-called separation fence. One Israeli response to the Intifada has been to construct a barrier approximately 500 miles long to attempt to seal off Israel from infiltration by terrorists. The fence includes electronic sensors, patrol roads, observation huts, and concrete walls reaching in some spots up to thirty feet in height. The Israeli budgets for 2004 and 2005 allocated $660 million for its construction, with the price tag expected to go higher.

Although supported in principle by a wide spectrum of Israeli politicians and public opinion, the fence too became a cause célèbre. It was coined a "Berlin wall–like barrier" in an open letter to President George W. Bush by sixteen retired U.S. foreign service officers criticizing of America's Mideast policy.

Vociferous international denunciation was met by many Israelis as proof that the world gleefully pounces upon Israel, while ignoring similar situations elsewhere. From my friend Aline I received a widely circulated e-mail with photos of security fences between Mexico and the U.S., North and South Korea, Spain and Morocco, India and Pakistan, cutting through Cyprus, and separating areas of Northern Ireland. The message concluded: "Only after we get rid of all these fences, one could ask Israel not to build a fence that protects her citizens from Palestinian terrorists."

Many predicted that the fence would become a de facto border, so its route was the focus of intense pressure from interested parties in the Israeli and Palestinian camps. Until actually in place, the exact location of the fence is subject to change. The barrier's route did not follow the Green Line of the state's 1949 borders. Some of it was to be constructed on Palestinian land conquered in 1967, and in places it cut through Palestinian villages or separated villagers from their fields.

In solidarity with adjacent Palestinians, some 200 Jewish residents of the Israeli town of Mevasseret Zion signed a petition against the route of the fence, which was to separate residents of the nearby village of Bet Surik from their fields and orchards. Mevasseret Zion, comprised of many professionals who commute to nearby Jerusalem, calls its relationship with the village "neighborly" and that the route would "upset the relative quiet that has existed between the two communities for some thirty-seven years." Approximately two dozen Mevasseret Zion residents joined in a court petition filed by Bet Surik and ten other Palestinian villages. On March 17, 2004, the High Court of Justice issued a stay delaying construction of the fence along the original route pending its final ruling. The court faced similar suits regarding other parts of the barrier.

When Palestinians began to demonstrate against the proposed route, Israeli activists like Ascherman came to their aid. I had followed Ascherman from afar and am on the RHR mailing list. On Wednesday April 14, 2004, I received an e-mail:

> There will be a demonstration in Bido on Thursday. We will leave from Liberty Bell Garden's parking lot [in Jerusalem] at 11:30. . . . We know that some of you do not want to be involved in standing in front of bulldozers. The demonstration will be arranged so that you can participate and express solidarity without standing in front of bulldozers, etc. It is terribly important that we prove that there is a sizable Israeli public, including those who support the idea of a barrier and are from the center of the political map, who are opposed to the current route of the Barrier.

Although tempted, I did not go, just as I have never gone to anything other than solidarity rallies in the relative safety of Tel Aviv.

What materialized was a far cry from Ascherman's hopeful projection. Tovah Lazaroff of the *Jerusalem Post* described the scene: "A lone Israeli woman . . . begged" the soldiers to show restraint, calling out:

"This is the only option we have to show the Israelis and the Palestinians there doesn't have to be violence, that there can be joint activity. There are many people here who really believe that."

The soldiers, however, began to fire tear gas.

Lazaroff's report concluded, "It appeared that security forces sparked the violence," and that among people "dragged away" and arrested was the woman who had pleaded to refrain from violence.

In that demonstration in which hundreds participated, four of the at least twenty injured were Israelis; of the ten protesters arrested, four were Israelis, including Ascherman.

Ascherman wrote an impassioned and painful e-mail message describing his arrest and the roughing up and humiliation to which he was subjected. He wrote that he, a Palestinian man, a Swedish protester, and a 12-year-old Palestinian boy were detained for hours next to a tank and used as human shields against Palestinian stones thrown at the tank. The boy was tied to the grill of the windshield.

Violence continued in Bidu. On April 18 the army reported that 600 people rioted and threw stones. The army fired rubber bullets to disperse them. A young Palestinian man was killed.

On a Friday a few days later, as if nothing had happened, or perhaps in spite of what had happened, I received another e-mail from RHR:

> We are trying to organize to help with the wheat harvest. More
> details next week. Shabbat Shalom.
>
> Arik

I read these reports on my computer screen in the safety of my study, with the sun streaming through the windows, within view of a date palm and eucalyptus tree in my quiet garden. My trash can stood outside my gate awaiting pickup. White noise included the muffled sound of cars driving a little too fast over speed bumps. On the front steps my daily newspaper awaited wrapped in a protective plastic bag. "Mom, we have to take pictures of these!" my daughter pointed to the crimson geraniums, yellow and brown pansies, purple petunias, and orange nasturtium. The street was decorated with crisp blue and white flags flying in the breeze for the upcoming Independence Day.

Tear gas? Rubber bullets? Concrete walls thirty feet high? They could be a thousand miles away.

Perhaps nothing had happened personally to radicalize me, unlike Four Mothers, a group started by women with sons in the army who mounted the ultimately successful nationwide campaign for Israeli withdrawal from Lebanon. But mine could also be an excuse. Four hundred Israeli women of all ages and walks of life participate in the volunteer organization Machsom [Checkpoint] Watch, which aims to monitor Israeli behavior toward Palestinians at checkpoints. Some step out of neighborhoods and lifestyles like mine to travel to the Israeli checkpoints to soften soldiers' attitudes, to document what happens, and to report on their Web site what they have observed.

Arbor Day in Israel is no lip-service holiday. In a country whose legendary boast was that it "made the desert bloom," trees are revered, even if planting ceremonies today are mostly limited to schoolchildren. And in a region where land is the bottom line, trees may be the true calibrator of the struggle for peace.

Consider the olive tree. The Psalms extol children by comparing them to olive branches around the table of the fortunate, and the olive is sanctified by the Koran.

Twenty-one-year old Israeli peace activist Karen Assaf made an unlikely bootlegger. But in 2001 she became a not-for-profit middle-man smuggling contraband Palestinian olive oil into Israel. As the territories were sealed off, oil normally sold to Israel was blocked. Army roadblocks made commerce between villages all but impossible.

Drivers used dirt roads to collect the oil and smuggle it past checkpoints. Through notices posted on the Web sites of Israeli coexistence organizations, Assaf accepted prepaid orders from Israeli individuals who traveled to pick it up themselves from the basement of Peace Now. I was one of them.

One gallon cost about $25, and checks accumulated drop by drop.

Assaf admitted it was a symbolic shoestring operation. Still, the several thousand dollars Assaf's campaign generated was far from symbolic to villagers whose one-crop income dropped to almost nothing due to closure.

The dilapidated Tel Aviv headquarters of Peace Now mirrored the moribund movement it represented. Its offices were one flight up a dark stairwell in a ramshackle building ripe for bulldozing or renovation. There was no sign downstairs and the door was bolted with security locks. "We get threats," a worker shrugged. In the basement beside torn and wrinkled peace banners stood a table loaded with cans, jars, and jugs of thick, homemade, Palestinian olive oil smuggled from West Bank villages into Israel, each marked with a customer's name. Mine was one.

But what a small insignificant gesture mine was, that one gallon of oil. A negligible contribution: words, wishes, small donations.

Yet many Israeli supporters of coexistence find it hard to order oil from villages around Tul Karem, where two young Israelis were murdered in cold blood in January 2001. It was just a few months into the Intifada, and the two, who owned a restaurant in Tel Aviv, had gone to the occupied territories to buy ceramic decorations for the restaurant's terrace. They were attacked while eating hummus in a local restaurant.

Olives, central to Middle Eastern culture and economy, are a symbol of unhappy times.

In the past few seasons ripe olives have rotted unpicked on laden trees. A large percent of the harvest has been lost, not due to the vagaries of nature—neither drought nor early violent rains—but through the vandalism and sabotage of men. The harvest, the olive groves, and olive pickers themselves have become victims of seasons that killed so many people and with them perhaps the peace that olive branches symbolize.

Though they are Israel's sixth largest crop, technology has not caught up with olives. Although machines are now also used for harvesting, many olives are still picked by hand or the trees are beaten with sticks until the olives fall on a cloth spread out on the ground. It is labor intensive work and Israeli grove owners depended on Palestinian hands for picking. But the Intifada triggered a security ban on travel by the Arab laborers who live in the territories and used to cross over daily into Israel to work. The pickers lost their livelihood and there was no one to replace them.

Arabs who tried to harvest their own olives were subject to violence by revengeful settlers. Settlers are reported to have snuck into groves at night to decimate them. Pictures of gratuitous vandalism have been aired on Israeli TV.

The most glaring victims are the thousands of olive trees destroyed by the Israeli army. Trees beside roadsides provide cover for stone throwers and snipers, thus prompting a policy of chopping them down or digging them up to boost security against ambushes. Palestinians view this destruction as revenge and collective punishment, claiming that trees hundreds of yards from roads have been sacrificed. In some instances desperate farmers have sawed off the limbs of felled trees and replanted them, hoping they will take root.

Israeli officers, themselves raised on an ethos that considered trees close to holy, often feel shocked and ambivalent at the task they perform, but maintain that trees giving cover for murderous attacks must go. As common here, both sides are right, both sides are wrong, and everybody continues to suffer.

If oil from olives lit every lamp in the ancient world, in today's Middle East even olives have become a force of darkness. In Israel the olive color is most often seen on the uniforms of soldiers and, ironically, the Mount of Olives is a famous Jewish graveyard in Jerusalem. The hills of the Galilee are dotted with thousands of olive trees. From afar their beauty inspires a false tranquility, mimicking their luckier brothers growing in peaceable Delphi and Sardinia and Provence.

"Peace," wrote Shakespeare, "proclaims olives of endless age." The gnarled trees of Israel and Palestine must feel in their old roots that on this bloodied soil the proclamation will be long in coming. Olive trees live hundreds of years, so they can afford to have patience. The rest of us don't have that luxury.

I receive several mailings from peace groups, so that I know that no fewer than eight Mideast coexistence camps took place in North America in the summer of 2004. I know the date of court hearings where inductees face charges for refusing on grounds of conscience to serve in the Israeli army. I know the latest on peaces initiatives.

One was a hope born when the so-called Geneva Accords blazed onto the scene in the fall of 2003. This joint Israeli–Palestinian effort outlined a detailed peace plan proposing to create a two-state solution by dividing land based on mutual interests. A printed booklet of the text was mailed to every household in Israel, with the desire that masses of people would sign, but detailed instructions on how to voice acceptance did not follow. Despite great international publicity, the plan was slow to capture the national imagination. Beginning in April 2004, Geneva organizers ran free tours of controversial locations in Jerusalem to raise public consciousness and demonstrate that a solution was feasible.

One by one Palestinian leaders were scratched from the list of individuals with whom Israel felt it could conduct a dialogue. Yasser Arafat steadily descended to the status of a persona non grata with the Israelis. The Israeli mantra became: "There is no partner for peace." Yet throughout the Intifada, one influential Palestinian has continued to be on a cordial first-name basis with Israelis, doggedly pursuing dialogue.

In all my twenty years in the State of Israel I have personally known only two Arabs well enough to speak to at length. One of them is Jamal al-Durrah, the Palestinian worker who painted my house and tiled my bathroom. The other is Professor Sari Nusseibeh, the scion of one of the most prestigious families in the Middle East, a Palestinian from East Jerusalem who holds a doctorate in philosophy from Harvard University and is president of Al Quds Arab University in Jerusalem.

The Intifada has made both these men internationally famous. Both icons of the Palestinian cause in their own ways, they travel around the world speaking, giving interviews, being photographed. Yet neither knows the other, and will probably never do so.

Professor Sari Nusseibeh and I shared an international journalism prize in 2002. Nusseibeh had written about implementation of peace through reason. My article had nothing to do with political science, or sociology or theories of government: I had won the prize for my article about Jamal al-Durrah.

Sari Nusseibeh is the darling of the Israeli Left. He meets often with the cream of the Israeli who's who, who are flattered and happy to be in his company. Riding in the elevator at Tel Aviv University I once found myself beside two up-and-coming intellectual movers of the Labor Party. One, a university professor before becoming a member of parliament, was talking about a meeting at which "Sari" would also be present, and it would be good to mention something to "Sari." The name "Sari" rolled back and forth, as if nonchalantly, but with obvious fluffing of one's feathers to be on a first-name basis. Before German Foreign Minister Joshke Fischer began an address I attended at Tel Aviv University in 2001, he gave a special greeting to Nusseibeh in the audience. Shimon Peres described him as a very courageous man. David Remnick, editor of the *New Yorker*, chose to come to Israel to spend time with Nusseibeh and then write about their visit in the magazine.

Nusseibeh was hand-picked in 2001 by Arafat to be the Palestinian Authority's senior representative to Jerusalem. Yet Sari Nusseibeh is the most outspoken dove among the Palestinians. Just a few months after the Intifada erupted, Nusseibeh made a stunning public negation of the right of return, the most sacred cow of the Palestinian rhetoric.

The right of return is a Palestinian axiom held aloft since 1948. It is shorthand for the position that Palestinians who left or were chased out of Israel during the War of Independence and, to a lesser extent, during the 1967 Six-Day War must be allowed the option to return to their former homes, most of which are now in the heart of Jewish Israel.

This insistence on the right of return hits hardest at the heart of Israeli paranoia. "OK," say Israelis, "so they get a state. But what they really want is to come back to Jaffa, and Lod—and all over! There is just not enough room for us both."

In December 2001, speaking to an Israeli Labor Party conference in Tel Aviv, Nusseibeh declared it impractical for the Palestinians to demand both an independent state and the right to return to Israel. "I believe the Palestinians should recognize that the refugees should return to a Palestinian state, enabling them to build a new life. . . . We must exchange the old Palestinian dream for a new one, for the sake of the future." In the fall of 2002 he reiterated this stance in a joint document he issued with former chief of Israeli intelligence Ami Ayalon.

As much as this startling position found wide approval with Israelis, many Palestinians would not forgive him for it. In January 2003, for example, Nusseibeh was prevented by angry students from participating in a campus seminar at the An Najah University on the West Bank.

If some Arabs view him as a traitor, not all the Jews believe him either. In a *Jerusalem Post* article entitled "Is Nusseibeh a Con Man?" Isi Leibler questioned Nusseibeh's true colors: "The jury is still out as to whether Nusseibeh is sincere or duplicitous. . . . Nusseibeh's behavior does not imply 'moderate' dissent from Arafat. . . . At best he is a propagandist playing his role in a good cop, bad cop performance orchestrated by Arafat. At worst, he is a straightforward con man."

Well, if Nusseibeh is a con man, I fell for him hook, line, and sinker. When I first saw him he was wearing scuffed loafers and an old corduroy jacket over a turtleneck sweater and slacks—the epitome of the Western academic.

Like me, Nusseibeh was born in 1948, coinciding with the birth of the State of Israel. In my case, it is always easy to know on Israeli Independence Day what year of its independence is being celebrated. Nusseibeh, though, may call the year of his birth the "*nakba*," the shorthand Arabic word used by Palestinians for what happened in 1948. To them the birth of Israel was simply "the catastrophe."

As on the later occasion we met, he wore a bemused expression, smiled often, and spoke impeccable English in a mellifluous voice. His impression as a soft-spoken man of culture is strengthened by his full head of salt and pepper hair and the feeling he conveys of trying very hard to respect and please his listener. Yet Nusseibeh exudes as well the easy charm of the aristocracy. He has a grace and a presence that seem to come from a lifetime of being listened to. Through his very gentleness and seeming humility others stop and take notice. It is hard to see or hear Sari Nusseibeh and not come away liking him.

That's exactly what happened to me when I heard him speak in January 2002 in a private home in Savyon, Israel's most upscale suburb. I was among a group of about ninety people invited by the hosts, earnest people dismayed at the collapse of dialogue between Jews and Arabs. It is not unusual to invite politicians, professors, and celebrities to speak to a gathered assemblage of invited guests, usually culled from among the acquaintances of the hosts. But in the winter of 2002 when bombs were going off like firecrackers on the streets of Israel, inviting a Palestinian was definitely unique. That's why I went; even though I had heard his name, I had no clear idea of who Nusseibeh actually was.

Nusseibeh arrived by taxi from his home in East Jerusalem.

By then entrances to all public places were already manned by armed security guards. For twenty years Israelis have been used to their bags being checked when entering a supermarket or a movie theater or a concert hall. But now they were searched when going into any restaurant or café, all malls, banks, office buildings, bus stations, train platforms, beaches, swimming pools, health clinics, bowling alleys, or museums. In many places security personnel moved a sort of Geiger-counter wand over the entrant's torso too. Guests arriving at wedding halls were checked, and people who gave big parties at their home had begun to pay the extra expense of hiring security guards to stand outside the entrance to screen the incoming guests. With Israeli society shell shocked by bombs like the one that went off during a Bat Mitzvah, killing the girl's grandfather who had just minutes before been videotaped giving her a pair of earrings, nobody considered this security to be overkill. On the contrary, they began to expect it. Passing by uniformed men with fat revolvers peeking out of their back pockets had become an unremarkable fact of life. As a matter of fact, people got nervous when they didn't see a guard.

But on that Saturday morning in Savyon, nobody stood outside on the quiet, tree-lined street to check either the speaker or the guests. Perhaps there was a tacit agreement that this was such an extraordinary event, it stood outside the normal status quo. Or maybe it was embarrassment, like admitting that if people were checked, Nusseibeh and company would have to be checked too, which might be a personal affront. In any case, the morning was as cultured, refined, and peaceful as one might imagine a brunch at a don's house in Oxford to be. Security guards would definitely have stood out like sore thumbs. Nusseibeh had arrived with sketchily introduced companions: a middle-aged woman, a teenage girl, and a heavyset man who spoke little and may have been a bodyguard.

The living room, dining room, and screened porch were bursting with people on couches, upholstered divans, and folding chairs. Most of them were middle-aged professionals, many professors, doctors, lawyers, and even an ex-army general. I had come in late, when the host was already in the process of introducing Nusseibeh, and found a place at the back of the living room.

I had accepted the invitation with no clear thought about whether or not to take notes and write an article about the meeting. But within minutes of Nusseibeh's shambling up to the mike, shaking his head sheepishly, and beginning to speak, I fished my notebook out of my purse, stood up, and craned my head to catch every word, and was completely under his spell.

Nusseibeh is not a man to raise his voice or make ringing declarations. Yet he is a master of rhetoric. He captures his audience by telling a story. That day he told about driving on a crowded road and accidentally grazing a woman pedestrian. Nusseibeh got out of the car and ascertained that she seemed unhurt. He handed the woman his card, telling her to call him if she discovered some injury. After that, he drove away. Hearing this scenario was the first shock to Western ears, where every motorist is familiar with the cardinal rule of behavior when involved in an accident: never admit liability. His culture apparently operates on a different paradigm.

But that was not the point of Nusseibeh's story. He heard nothing from the woman and soon forgot the incident. Several weeks later, Nusseibeh's father asked him if perhaps he had hit someone with his car. Nusseibeh was astounded—his father had himself been contacted by people from the woman's village who reproached him about Nusseibeh's conduct.

What had Nusseibeh done wrong? How could he possibly be faulted? To Western eyes he had acted the perfect gentleman.

Nusseibeh's father, however, understood the complaint, even if his middle-aged son did not. And he took him to task for it. Having wronged the woman, even unintentionally, it was incumbent upon Nusseibeh to seek her out, to verbalize his sympathy for her, and by doing so, show that he accepted responsibility. But as it was, the woman's family felt a mounting sense of having been wronged. They suspected that Nusseibeh, from a well-known aristocratic family, didn't want to demean himself by coming to her simple village.

Although the woman was indeed uninjured physically, the accident spawned escalating hurt feelings. The gesture of public apology and acceptance of responsibility was expected.

Nusseibeh used this experience as a metaphor for the Israeli–Palestinian impasse. He believes that for Palestinians it is essential that Israel make public acknowledgment to the Palestinians that the birthing process of Israeli statehood caused them injury, even if unintentionally. Until Israel is ready to make this psychological leap, Palestinian anger and resentment will fester.

Such an opportunity nearly arose shortly before that day when Israeli President Moshe Katsav expressed readiness to address the Palestinian parliament in the West Bank city of Ramallah to voice regret over the loss of lives on both sides and request a year-long cease-fire. Arafat reportedly was amenable, but Prime Minister Sharon nixed the plan. Katsav, whose position as president is largely ceremonial, had no choice but to yield.

Nusseibeh termed Katsav's proposal of a symbolic visit to Palestinians a gesture of "genius," which would have gone "right to Palestinian hearts." It would have been an overture similar to the one Nusseibeh should have made on a much smaller scale with the woman he had hit with his automobile.

But on that morning Nusseibeh was not pessimistic. He ended his talk saying: "There is no reason to feel that we have to reach 100 percent agreement; if we reach 10, 20, 30 percent, we can congratulate ourselves."

The next time I would hear Sari Nusseibeh speak I wouldn't be taking notes from the audience. Six months later he and I would be sitting side by side on a podium in the European Parliament in Belgium.

In the winter of 2002 a peace rally still attracted thousands, at which Arabs participated as well. The lyrics of John Lennon rose in the night air of Tel Aviv: "You may say that I'm a dreamer but I'm not the only one . . ." The words rang out in both Hebrew and Arabic in a square ringed by the city's art museum, central library, and courthouse. Called in support of Israeli army officers who declared they would refuse to serve in the occupied territories, 10,000 Arabs and Jews joined together holding high their black placards, "The Occupation Is Killing Us All." A plaintive Israeli ballad took on new meaning when it was sung in the original juxtaposed with its Arabic translation, expressing the passion and tragedy of both nationalities: "I have no other country—even if my land is burning."

Shulamit Aloni, the grande dame of Israel's civil rights movement, recited a poem by one of the country's foremost national poets about how a soldier must retain his humanity in wartime. During Israel's War of Independence in 1948, she said, this poem by Natan Alterman was distributed to every soldier in the Israeli army. In today's climate would the poet be called a clarion for justice—or dismissed as a fringe spokesman of the "extreme Left"?

A few months later, in May 2002, I traveled to another peace rally with a 44-year-old Israeli who could be called the father of army refuseniks. Yuval Lotam served two jail terms for refusing to do military service in the occupied territories. It was Lotam's first time in many years at a rally.

"I always mean to go, but somehow I never get moving in time," he told me, looking sheepish.

Lotam melted into the crowd of 60,000. As a young soldier Lotam served three years as an officer in the paratroopers. Then he experienced an about-face of conscience, and for the ensuing twenty years refused reserve duty in the land occupied by his country. The army "just didn't know what to do with an officer like me," he told me. But in 1993 and again in 1997 he was sentenced to twenty-eight days in a military prison.

Retiring, soft-spoken Lotam refused to get mileage out of his actions. "I am probably the most selfish refusenik ever," he claimed. "The only reason I do it is for myself, so I can bear to look in the mirror."

Lotam was more loquacious on the subject of the friendships with Palestinians that evolved from his act. In 1997 Lotam's imprisonment stemmed from his refusal to perform guard duty at a prison housing administrative detainees. In a carryover from British colonial rule, Israel holds security suspects in detention for renewable intervals of up to six months without bringing specific charges against them. Immad Sabi, a Palestinian administrative detainee at the prison Lotam refused to guard, saw a small newspaper notice reporting Lotam's imprisonment, and wrote him an open letter. Sabi's letter, eventually published in the *New York Times* in July 1997, touched off a friendship between the two men. Later as a graduate student living in Holland, Sabi hosted Lotam at his home.

After his release in 1997 Lotam helped initiate a program of personal correspondence between Israelis and administrative detainees, and he remained in contact with several. "These days my friends in

Ramallah and Jenin urge me to do something. When I ask 'What can I do?' they say, 'At least go to the rallies!'" So this time Lotam made the effort.

My acquaintance with Lotam began when I saw Lotam himself written up in the *New York Times* in August 1997. Stunned to read that he lived in the same little town that I do, I looked him up and went to visit. When I drove to the rally, I invited Lotam to accompany me.

Standing near the stark granite slab that marks the spot where Yitzhak Rabin was assassinated at the peace rally in the same square in 1995, Lotam listened to the speakers on the podium.

Ala Shainskaya, a scientist who emigrated from the former Soviet Union twelve years earlier, hesitated when invited to be a speaker— until people asked her if she wasn't afraid participation might jeopardize her job at a prestigious scientific institute. "That decided me," she said in heavily accented Hebrew. "I came here from a totalitarian regime. I refuse to let this happen to our democratic country." To Shainskaya the emphasis on togetherness at any price may engender suppression of dissent. "What does 'togetherness' mean?" she asked. "That we all must think alike and march alike like robots?"

Similar thoughts twenty years ago motivated Lotam to begin his "selective" refusal. As the Intifada progressed, the movement to refuse service gathered steam. Some were pure pacifists opposed to all military service; some pinpointed their refusal to serve in the occupied territories. They came from all sectors, including high school students approaching induction age, pilots, reservists, and draftees. Open letters by pilots and high-ranking army reservists raised a furor among the public. As of June 2004 the Refuser Solidarity Network posted this update on their Web site: "1347 say no, 1347 won't go," and five who refused induction were serving one-year prison sentences.

But refusal to serve has been condemned across the Israeli political spectrum, and brought up difficult philosophical and practical choices for many young people, even for those who oppose Israel's current policies. Going to the army after high school is the natural course for most young men and women. My town holds an annual evening of commendation and farewell for all local youth about to be conscripted. In mainstream Israeli society, those who do not serve in the army—for whatever reason—may be looked at askance. Serving in any capacity in this citizen's army is part of the society's credentials, and being in an "elite" unit often opens doors later on. Prime Ministers Sharon, Barak, and Rabin were army generals before entering politics. So was former Haifa Mayor Avram Mitzna, who, as the Labor Party candidate for prime minister, unsuccessfully tried to topple Sharon on a peace platform in 2003. Benjamin Netanyahu served in the most prestigious selective unit.

Thus, if not the sacred cow it once was, the army is still one of the pillars of Israel. Refusing to serve may have long-term practical implications.

One of my law students missed weeks of school in 2002 after being called up to his reserve unit where he served as a tank commander. In an article in a student newsletter analyzing in legal and moral terms his opposition to a refusal-to-serve petition, he termed it unjustified defiance to exploit the cloak of the military to express one's ideology. Likewise, the Israeli Supreme Court has ruled in the past that exemptions from army service may be granted for reasons of conscience, but that selective refusal based on opposition to specific policies is illegitimate.

Twenty-eight-year-old David Damelin was another called up for reserves. The philosophy student was a regular at peace demonstrations, but when his activist mother urged him to sign an officers' petition against service in the territories, he declined. Damelin reported for duty—and was killed in a Palestinian attack on an army checkpoint in 2002. Sixty days after his death Damelin's mother somberly addressed the rally: "The suffering of Palestinian mothers and Israeli mothers is the same. Put yourselves in the other's place." On her son's fresh gravestone were carved the words of poet Kahlil Gibran: "All the earth is his birthplace and all mankind his brothers."

Yuval Lotam listened, nodding. He left the rally as anonymously as he had come. "I'm no kind of hero," he insisted.

The Peace Now organization used to draw tens of thousands of mainstream Israelis to its demonstrations. Slowly, with the despondent peace camp in disarray, the demonstrations petered out. But in May 2004, three and a half years into the Intifada, 150,000 demonstrators poured into Rabin Square. I too felt I could not stay away, and I listened all afternoon to radio reports of which streets would be closed for security. Since the debacle of Rabin's assassination, when anybody could drive right in, the police no longer took chances. I drove to Tel Aviv with my friend Mazal, parked a couple of blocks away, and obligingly opened my bag for inspection at the police cordons ringing the square.

The rally came upon the heels of one of Israel's blackest weeks, when thirteen soldiers were killed in Gaza. Withdrawal from the Gaza Strip was the theme of the rally. It had been planned in advance, but after the soldiers were killed, voices on the right urged that the rally be canceled, calling it a desecration of their fresh graves. But the organizers persisted, and began the evening with a minute of silence in their memory. The speakers included the big names like Shimon Peres and Yossi Beilin.

But standing in the overflowing crowd and craning my neck to see, I was mesmerized by a most unexpected speaker—Yom Tov Samia, none other than the major general in charge of Gaza during the shooting of Jamal al-Durrah and the death of his son Mohammed. From what I remembered, Samia's attitude could be characterized as anything but pacific. Yet there he was on the peace podium, dressed in civilian clothes because he had since left the military, declaring, "Time is not in our favor. We have been in Gaza for thirty-seven years, and as time goes by the solution will only grow more difficult." If Samia had joined the voices calling for Israeli withdrawal, albeit a gradual one, then, I felt, the handwriting was finally on the wall.

At that rally on a spring night I saw young and old, people in wheelchairs, fathers carrying toddlers on their shoulders, happy young couples, even elderly with canes. Finally the people had come back out to the streets.

The rally wrapped up with the singing of the Israeli national anthem, "Hatikva" ("The Hope"). It was led by an 18-year-old girl in the twelfth grade. Two springs before she had been one of the wounded in the Dolphinarium bombing. Now she was calling for peace.

Anybody who wants to visit the recently christened Mountain of Israeli–Palestinian Friendship will not find it in the Middle East. Scaled by a team of four Israelis and four Palestinians in January 2004, it stands as far away on the planet as one can get—on the lonely continent of Antarctica. Organized by the charity Extreme Peace Missions with involvement from the Peres Center for Peace, the team sailed from southern Chile for 15 days through ice and storms to Antarctica. The mission was the brainchild of Heskel Nathaniel, an expatriate Israeli businessman. Nathaniel read the team's statement upon the summit:

> We, the members of Breaking the Ice, the Israeli–Palestinian expedition to Antarctica, having reached the conclusion of a long journey by land and sea from our homes in the Middle East to the southernmost reaches of the earth, now stand atop this unnamed mountain. By reaching its summit we have proven that Palestinians and Israelis can cooperate with one another with mutual respect and trust. . . . We join together in rejecting the use of violence in the solution of our problems and hereby declare that our peoples can and deserve to live together in peace and friendship. In expression of these beliefs and desires we hereby name this mountain "The Mountain of Israeli–Palestinian Friendship."

The stunning expedition of Breaking the Ice was greeted in Santiago, Chile, by emotional crowds of local Arabs and Jews, some brought together for the first time by the event. Members of the team were interviewed on National Public Radio, written up in the world media, covered by CNN and the BBC, and were met and encouraged by United Nations Secretary General Kofi Annan and the Dalai Lama.

In contrast, although some mention of the expedition made Israeli press and television, it did not succeed in firing the collective imagination. When I asked Allon Bar of the Peres Center how to account for this he answered, "The Israeli media is more cynical."

Heskel Nathaniel had the same reaction, but explained it to me this way: "In Israel who knows what will happen next week? They don't have time and attention for what's symbolic. Israelis want to see immediate results. And our expedition was symbolic."

"Do you see any practical results?"

"None of us is naive enough to believe that after coming back from Antarctica we would see a new reality. It was a drop in the ocean, but it was our personal drop.

"Some people can write. Some people can sing," Nathaniel went on. "We climbed mountains . . ."

Without the possibility of interchange it is but a small step to collective demonization of the other. A one-of-a-kind social experiment attempted to pierce the soundproof curtain that descended on dialogue between individuals in Israel on the one hand and Gaza and the West Bank on the other. Not between politicians. Not between delegations. Not between professional groups. Not between celebrities. With supreme—and perhaps naive—faith in the common man, the binational organization Israeli–Palestinian Bereaved Parents for Peace conceived a grass roots connection of the most basic and immediate kind, a scheme to allow Palestinians and Israelis a first step in one-to-one contact: It simply gave them the opportunity to talk.

With its project "Hello, Salaam! Hello, Shalom! Hello, Peace!" the group initiated an audacious program by employing the lowest common denominator of communication: the telephone.

For although Israelis and Palestinians are now unable to meet in person, telephone lines between them are as open as a conversation between two teenagers living in adjacent apartments. Israelis and Palestinians may be in places blocked off and inaccessible from one another, but their cell phones have identical area codes.

But how would anybody from either side know whom to contact within the sea of the other nationality?

Hello, Peace! established an ingenious matrix for telephone contact: an automated telephone system routed through a central number. Any individual could talk without charge to a member of the other side.

When instituted in the autumn of 2002, the project was advertised on billboards and in the Israeli and Arabic press. Its existence spread by word of mouth. By April 2004 organizers reported over 400,000 calls had been made.

In theory the idea sounded intriguing to me and I decided to try it. It took determination and perseverance to get through.

The category I specified to contact were women between the ages of 30 and 60. Out of the twenty-nine entries in this category, and after nearly half an hour on the phone I was able to reach only two. The first I was unable to converse with, as she spoke two languages I didn't know, Arabic and Spanish. The most I could manage to stumble out was "Gracias, Salaam." The second, Hasam from Ramallah, told me repeatedly how bad the situation was, how all contacts she had had with Israeli peace groups had been severed. Mine was the first call from Israel she had received. I finished our talk with the words, "Maybe someday we will meet in Ramallah." Hasam replied, "Or in Tel Aviv!"

But actually, I was not entirely candid. I had indeed spent a day visiting Ramallah in the spring of 2000. Even then, it was not a journey to be undertaken without second thoughts. My American-born poet friend Janice and I joined my friend Carol in her car with diplomatic license plates. The people we met were mostly friendly, but we didn't exactly walk around with Hebrew lettering on our T-shirts. Also, we made a point to speak English. Traveling around the town by car and on foot, we wound up our visit at a late lunch in a local restaurant.

There I met a local photographer who was to participate in an exhibit in Tel Aviv. Would I mail a negative of his to the gallery when I got back to Israel? Sure, I agreed. He handed me the envelope unsealed. I wondered why, but he was more savvy than I—if I was to mail it, I should be sure of what it contained. On our way back to the car we passed a giant painted graffiti upon a wall. An Arab translated it for me: "Jerusalem is ours." The slogan's defiant conviction prompted Janice to write a prescient pessimistic poem about what the future held.

Then in October 2000, a few weeks into the Intifada, two Israeli soldiers who strayed into Ramallah were lynched and mutilated by a local mob. The television played the shots of the lifeless body of one being dumped head first from the second floor of the Palestinian police station where he had been beaten and stabbed to death. Battered and stomped by a surging mob reported to be over 1000, the corpse was set alight and dragged through the streets. I saw the shot of one jubilant man in the window displaying raised palms smeared with fresh crimson blood—a victory salute of hatred.

For me that ferocious picture is the most personally frightening of the Intifada. The lynching in Ramallah reminded me of nothing so much as the terrible lynching photographs from the American past I had seen the previous summer in an exhibition in New York—exultant spectators and participants beside limp, battered, lifeless victims. The exhibit had generated controversy in New York: Were the pictures too cruel and graphic to be shown? Now photos of lynching were no longer history. No matter what happens, it will take a very long time before I myself will ever willingly return to Ramallah.

My conversation with Hasam showed me that even when there is a human being on the other end, it is not always easy to break the ice with a stranger and exchange more than platitudes. But the very fact of any conversation at all is in itself of significance, although perhaps limited to the symbolic.

Determined to make further contact, I myself set up a message box leaving my name and a greeting of welcome in English. Within a few hours and continuing over several months, I received calls. Most were from young men; none from women. Unfortunately, the language barrier proved difficult to breach. Caller after caller spoke only Arabic.

Then I received a call from Ahmed from Hebron. He, like all us callers, identified himself only on a first-name basis. Ahmed and I conversed in Hebrew, which he had learned during his many years working in Israel as a building subcontractor.

He had talked with many Israelis through this telephone project, some of them several times.

"Do you think these calls can help?" I asked him. "What can you and I accomplish by talking together? What actually can an individual do?"

Ahmed answered, "It is true, I can do nothing. But Israelis can. Israel is a democracy. Israel has all the power on its side. The scales are not even. Israelis are the ones who can make a choice."

When I asked Ahmed what message he would give to Israelis if he could, he said without hesitation, "To know that we too deserve to live like human beings."

"Are you working now?" I asked.

"Not now," he answered. "Now the situation is terrible."

"So what do you do?"

"What do I do?" He laughed. "I sit at home and watch television—and I talk on the phone."

Similar to other societies in crisis, the arts in Israel—books, plays, and the visual arts—seem consumed by the conflict. Above all, Israeli films agonize over the trauma. Not all the films, though, are tragic. Among the most touching was a small masterpiece, *Promises*, shown at festivals around the world and on American television as well as in Israel. In 1998, during the high noon of the peace process, Israeli-born filmmaker B. Z. Goldberg and his collaborator, Justine Shapiro, traced the lives of young Israeli and Palestinian teenagers. Among them were: Faraj, from the Daheishe refugee camp, who carried the key to his grandparents house razed after the 1948 war; Sanabel, a girl from Daheishe, who danced dances of Palestinian liberation;

Moishe, a boy from a Jewish settlement on the West Bank; Mahmoud, son of an Arab coffee merchant in East Jerusalem; and finally, Yarko and Daniel, the vibrant and sensitive Israeli twins.

During the filming, the children formed an emotional tie to Goldberg. Mahmoud, his fingers intertwined with Goldberg's, was unable to accept the director's Israeli background. "You are not an authentic Jew," he insisted. The children also became increasingly more curious about their counterparts. Using the director's cell phone, they began hesitant conversations and eventually the twins went to visit Faraj and Sanabel. They played soccer together and were guests for a festive meal. Everybody I knew who saw the film fell in love with it and with its young participants.

But *Promises*, which seemed to make a real promise, followed the sad pattern of the Middle East. Two years after their first and only meeting Sanabel stared darkly into the camera and said: "Life won't let us accomplish our dreams." In the spring of 2002 some of the *Promises* children traveled to the United States to attend the Academy Awards ceremony, where the film had been nominated for best documentary. But by then the Intifada had done its work on them too. Faraj's brother-in-law had been killed. Interviewed by Bob Simon on CBS television, an embittered and radicalized Sanabel stared coldly into the camera and declared: "I want to be a suicide bomber." Even if it were possible to meet again, Sanabel had turned her back. "I am not willing to see a Jewish person," she said. "Because they are all the same. They are all racists. They are all evil." When I heard the new Sanabel, it was hard not to conclude that any and all promises were erased. The film did not win an Oscar.

In April 2004 my husband and I managed to get tickets with friends to a sold-out matinee showing of the Israeli-made documentary *Checkpoint* at the Tel Aviv International Documentary Film Festival. Directed by Israeli Yoav Shamir and filmed by an Israeli crew, *Checkpoint* is a look by Israelis at the moral labyrinth into which the Intifada has plunged them.

The film had also been chosen to open the festival, and was thereafter screened on Israeli television. *Checkpoint* depicts encounters between Israeli soldiers manning dozens of security crossings around the West Bank created during the Intifada to help thwart terrorist attacks, and the thousands of ordinary Palestinians who must pass through them in order to go about their lives. The festival called it a portrayal of the "harsh and banal routine . . . that form[s] a microcosm of the Occupation." And *Checkpoint* was indeed a harsh film to watch.

There were relatively few instances of deliberate humiliation, but many scenes showed a reality that in itself epitomizes degradation. Palestinians shivered without shelter in cold and rain while soldiers took hours to check their documents. The elderly stood on line exhausted. A mother allowed to pass only by herself had to send her small children to return alone by foot to their village; as they cried and clung to her, she pushed them away, scolding in desperation, "Go on now, before the soldier changes his mind and doesn't let me pass either!" Schoolchildren had to descend while their bus was searched on their way to school and again in the afternoon upon return. Even ambulance passengers en route to the hospital were checked.

But Israeli viewers could recall recent news reports of Palestinian children sent across checkpoints as human sacrifices—strapped with explosive belts that would have blown them up along with their intended victims. They might have heard the report of a woman let through after feigning a leg implant who then detonated her bomb and killed four, and of weapons concealed within ambulances. Because here in the Middle East, for every injustice one shows, the other side can retort with a corresponding horror.

The decision to be allowed to pass was often at the individual soldier's discretion and sometimes seemed arbitrary—a truck driver was turned away, while a man going to visit his bride before their wedding was let through. The young soldier, obviously identifying with the bridegroom, said to his buddy, "What could I do? It was his *wedding*."

The audience sat in what seemed like stunned silence as the film unrolled. Sometimes I heard gasps and murmurs of disquiet. Afterward in the lobby I recognized several acquaintances. All were visibly upset by the degradation they had seen.

Checkpoint was screened in the heart of Tel Aviv, in an area surrounded by cafés, upscale furniture stores, art museum and opera, doctors' clinics, and the Chamber of Commerce. Outside on that day, refreshment stands sold Murphy's ale and bands played Irish music in honor of an Irish arts festival.

Yet around the outdoor plaza police barriers were in place, and every moviegoer was searched by armed guards carrying sensor devices. It was as if every Israeli too had to pass through his own checkpoint, a checkpoint so routine that few give it more than a passing glance.

But if security checkpoints have become part of the warp and woof of Israeli life, they are of an incomparably minor dimension compared to the checkpoints of Palestinians.

The word *Intifada* in Arabic does not mean rebellion, fight, or revolt. It means "a shaking off of fleas." This graphic, unappealing metaphor can fit many Israelis' feelings as well, who just wish the seemingly unsolvable problem would go away.

They daily shake off the existential situation in which they find themselves mired. Scenes in *Checkpoint* made me tremble. I believe they made hundreds—perhaps thousands—of Israelis viewers tremble.

But as I went out onto the streets of Tel Aviv, I heard the festive Irish music and saw the stands selling Murphy's Ale. Our friends asked us to join them for a drink. The problem is not that we don't care, but that we push our caring to the back of our minds all too soon.

Poet Natan Yonatan, who never stopped caring, was a symbol of an Israel that no longer exists. The people's poet from a strong socialist background who published twenty volumes of poetry, he was never fully accepted by the intellectual establishment. But the man in the street loved him, and many of his poems were set to popular music. One became the emblem of the assassinated Prime Minister Yitzhak

Rabin: "Where Can Be Found More People Like That Man?" When I heard the announcement in March 2004 that Israel's gentle poet had passed away, it was this line that played over and over in my head. I remembered Yonatan for the humanity and vision he radiated the two times we met, meetings separated by a gap of thirty-four years.

The radio reported that Yonatan was 81 at his death. Quickly I did the arithmetic: When I first met him in 1967 the silver-haired, silver-tongued poet already seemed a sage. Yet he must have been just 44.

In the heady days after Israel's lightning victory in the Six-Day War, I was a rookie summer counselor in a Jewish youth camp in New York State. Although the camp was normally of a middle-of-the-road philosophy, that summer in the wake of what was perceived as the averted annihilation of Israel, the flush of victory made the counselors' and campers' blood rise. "Rabin is waiting for Nasser!" they chanted in unison, pounding out victory dances and raising fists: "On to Damascus!"

I and my friends and family had spent the black month preceding the war in terror, our fear rising with every passing day for the state's very existence. Then all at once little Israel seemed invincible, and the spirit of the camp was one of rousing chauvinism. But I stood on the outside, repelled by the jingoistic slogans and the glorification of battle swirling around me.

Word came that an Israeli emissary would visit to give a talk on his perceptions of the war. I expected stories of battle glories and praise for the newborn Greater Israel.

But when Natan Yonatan got up to speak, his mellifluous voice was choked with sorrow. He spoke not of the glory of battle, but of its tragedy, of the losses on both sides, and how perhaps this war would be a start toward a rapprochement between the two peoples. Yonatan's electrifying words came a decade before Egyptian president Sadat's visit to Jerusalem made the first crack in the ice and over a quarter of a century before the Oslo peace accords. They came as well six years before his own 21-year-old son was killed on the first day of the Egyptian attack on Israel in October 1973.

Yonatan lived his poetry in his life. He persisted in his beliefs even after his son's death, in whose memory he published the volume *Stones in the Darkness*. Yonatan was buried in the section of the cemetery reserved for parents of fallen soldiers.

I came face to face with Yonatan again in 2002 at a poetry reading celebrating the publication of my friend Janice's book of poems. Before me I saw an old man, but his melodious voice and sad velvet eyes had not changed. This time, we met at the height of the Intifada, yet Yonatan still clung stubbornly to his vision.

He related his strong ties to the head of the Palestinian Writers Union in Ramallah, who, like himself, was a bereaved father. Yonatan had accompanied the poet to the son's grave, which bore a marker extolling the young man killed by Israelis. Yonatan told me sadly that the Intifada had accomplished its task: his contact with the Palestinian poet had been interrupted by the bloodshed. But Yonatan did not lose hope. It was only temporary, he insisted. The day would return when words of peace would ring out not only in poets' words on paper, but throughout the streets.

Natan Yonatan did not live to see that day come. But when it does, Yonatan and other tireless unsung people of commitment will be on its roll of honor.

Chapter Ten *Celebrity for One Night*

At the Hotel Leopold in Brussels, exquisitely packaged chocolates nestle in transparent refrigerated display cases. The dates of freshness are stamped on gift boxes of truffles, pralines, nougats, and orange slices dipped in bitter chocolate. There are bonbons in the shape of curled sea shells and autumn leaves that look more like works of art than candy. A Hershey bar left in the fridge will soon sprout an unappealing white film, but in the kingdom of chocolate the venerable Belgian brands—Godiva, Leonides, and Neuhaus—chill their treasures to preserve the fresh cream used in their fabrication. Although trivia mavens may cite Switzerland as the land of chocolate, the Belgians are confident the true connoisseur knows their national treasure is unrivaled.

Belgian food is like French cuisine cum laude. From airy croissants to steak au poivre, the saying goes that it is impossible to eat a bad meal in Belgium.

I can't vouch for its truth, though, because for most of the two days I spent in Brussels I was too queasy to have an appetite. The one festive meal I did eat was memorable for the company around the table.

I touched down in Belgium on a day in early summer when the city was a green paradise of leafy trees and blooming flowers. It felt like an oasis after Israel. Home of the European Parliament and the seat of the European Union, Brussels reminded me of Washington or Geneva.

My hotel was a stone's throw from sleek new buildings where the policy and paperwork of the new united Europe churn. The streets were filled with rising young functionaries in suits with slicked hair and eager faces. They carried slim attaché cases whose leather hadn't had a chance to scuff, and the women wore soft blouses with silk scarves knotted at the neck, knee-length straight skirts, shiny stockings, and patent leather pumps. As they exited one building and strode purposefully toward the next, stopping to chat before revolving doors, their faces wore the expressions of the youngish middle-aged trying hard to convince that they are people on the rise. Even though temporarily not behind their desks or at the phone, they made sure that all who might see them would understand that here was an under secretary or an economics expert or a statistician whose star was definitely ascending.

I arrived in Brussels on June 25, 2002, five months after the phone rang one January evening in my home. As I listened to what a young woman told me—that I had won a journalism prize—I thought it was like the bogus calls announcing that you have won some fantastic far-away sweepstakes and all that you need do is to come and collect the reward.

But the friendly American caller introduced herself as Taly Lind and said she was calling from Jerusalem representing a Washington-based international conflict-resolution organization called Search for Common Ground. She told me a *Jerusalem Post* article I had written, "That boy who wore my hand-me-downs," had been awarded the 2001 Common Ground Award for Journalism in the Middle East.

"But that was published in 2000," I blurted out.

"Yes, but the controlling dates are not precise, and the judges chose your article."

I stammered that I was not familiar with Common Ground, and as I spelled out my e-mail to her, Lind promised to send me a message including the organization's Web site.

I put down the phone and called out, "Guess what!" My daughters were overjoyed, waltzing me around the room, but I retained a reservation of incredulity until the next day when a message from Taly Lind really did appear in my in-box. And with it, the Web site of the Search for Common Ground.

I learned that the organization headquartered in Washington had offices in troubled corners of the globe, including Macedonia and Angola. And last but not least, in Jerusalem. And yes, they indeed awarded an annual journalism prize to articles from the Middle East that embodied their theme of reconciliation: a winner from the Arab press, a winner from the Israeli press, and a winner from the foreign press. The Search for Common Ground was for real. The prize was no hoax, and it was apparently no hoax that I had won.

Versions of my article about Jamal al-Durrah had been published in the *Boston Globe* and by *Salon.com*, so I wondered whether Lind meant I was the recipient of the prize from the Western press. But she had mentioned the title that a *Jerusalem Post* editor had pinned on the column I had sent in under the name "Our Jamal." If it was that hand-me-down article, then indeed I had been picked to represent the Israeli press.

The *Jerusalem Post* has been publishing for over seventy-five years. Its original name before Israel's statehood was the *Palestine Post*, and this was the name printed on the pay vouchers that for four and a half years arrived for my opinion column every fortnight.

Despite press releases sent to all the Israeli papers, the *Jerusalem Post* made no mention of the prize I had won in its name or of the award ceremony.

Haaretz newspaper, however, did find it fit to cover the award. It too had been the home of an article by one of the winners, for Sari Nusseibeh's article was reprinted in *Haaretz* in Hebrew translation after it had first appeared in the Arabic language Jerusalem newspaper *Al Quds*.

The award ceremony was set for the evening of June 26. I arrived the morning before.

Then I spent the day and a half after my arrival walking through Brussels' leafy streets, sitting on benches in public parks, in the Grand Place, near palaces and museums. In all these places I practiced the speech I had written for the prize ceremony, addressing the trees, or elderly couples walking dogs, or exuberant high school students streaming out of school into the bright June sunshine.

One of my stops was the Israeli embassy. I had been told that the award ceremony was to be composed of speeches by EU Commissioner of Foreign Relations Christopher Patten, who would present the awards, followed by five-minute speeches by each award winner. Sari Nusseibeh, I was told, would be speaking longer on the tactics of nonviolence in the vein of Mahatma Gandhi and Martin Luther King, Jr. Hearing that didn't do anything for my jitters. I saw myself up on the platform not only with the famous Nusseibeh but with the ghosts of the legendary King and Gandhi. Then would come a press conference where politicians and the press were to pose questions to those on the podium.

In the spring of 2002 the Israeli press was full of stories outlining the rise of European anti-Semitism and the increasingly anti-Israeli stance of European countries and organizations, especially Belgium and the European Union. The prospect of answering possibly hostile questions in a public forum filled me with apprehension. As the winner from the Israeli press category, as a woman who lived in Israel, I felt I myself would be seen as representing the State of Israel. I was no seasoned public speaker, and was worried how I might tackle hostile questions that put me in the mode of defending or explaining the policies of the State of Israel as a spokesperson of the country.

Before my trip I therefore telephoned both the Israeli Foreign Ministry and the Israeli embassy in Brussels. I wanted them to brief me as to what to expect and how to handle it. Bemused officials in Jerusalem passed me from person to person, until at last a kind official told me to fend off any hostile questions with the disclaimer that I was a private individual representing only myself, and to develop a set line to respond to a questioner's anger.

The Israeli embassy in Brussels was reluctant to take me seriously as well. To my first long-distance telephone call announcing that I would be coming to town to accept a coexistence journalism prize and would like to speak to the press attaché, the response was that he was out of the office and generally busy hosting high-level guests from Israel. Prizes and award ceremonies, it turns out, are pretty much a dime a dozen in Brussels, and my arrival did not exactly galvanize the enthusiasm of the Israeli representatives in Belgium.

However, I felt the need for some solidarity and preparation, and kept phoning. I was finally able to get in touch with Chaim Assaraf, the spokesman for the Israeli mission to the European Union. Assaraf agreed to meet me and invited me to come to his office the afternoon I arrived.

So two hours after I checked into the Hotel Leopold I asked the concierge for a city map and began to hunt for the location of the Israeli embassy. To no avail, the street did not appear. When I turned to the concierge for help, he looked at the slip of paper in my hand and exclaimed, "Of course that street is not on our city map! It is in Onkel!" The Israeli embassy was located far from the center of town. Neither buses nor trams offered easy access. A twenty-minute taxi ride, I was told, was my only alternative.

I walked to a busy intersection, and entered a teeming cafe. As usual when just arriving abroad, I noted happily that no armed guard sat at the door to check the contents of my purse. The coffee in even the simplest coffee shop in Brussels is delicious, and is always served with a square of Belgian chocolate on the saucer. But I noticed that the waiter was distracted, and indeed the café was filled to capacity, although it was midafternoon on a work day. All eyes were on a large television screen mounted on the wall, and every few minutes the air was pierced by cheers and exclamations. The patrons, the chefs, and the waiters were all focused on a soccer game on the screen. This was no ordinary day. I had come to Brussels at the height of the World Soccer Cup. I looked enviously at their lightheartedness.

Leaving the cafe I hailed a cab and, speaking French, told the driver discreetly I wanted to go to Onkel. "Oh," he exclaimed before I had a chance to give the street address, "so you're going to the Israeli embassy!"

I was taken aback. "How did you *know*?"

"Most everybody who takes a cab to Onkel has that as his destination." So much for traveling incognito.

The Israeli embassy is situated on a tiny quiet residential street. It occupies a private villa surrounded by a high white wall. A Belgian police car is stationed at the end of the short block. To get to the door I first had to answer questions put to me in Hebrew by a friendly Ethiopian-Israeli guard outside. Inside there were two vestibules; I gained access to the second only after satisfactorily answering the questions of a receptionist behind a glass partition.

Chaim Assaraf greeted me warmly. He was an expansive man who looked like he enjoyed the good life abroad. But, he told me, what they say about Belgian anti-Semitism is no joke. It's even an understatement. However, Assaraf did not share my apprehensions about being grilled at the ceremony.

"They are usually very polite at occasions like these," he said. "Just think of some points you want to make, and stick to them if they ask you questions," he said. "Don't feel pressured into answering what you don't want to. And your best position is that you are a private individual, a writer, and not a politician or spokesperson. Anyway, I will be there in the audience to support you."

I wasn't totally pacified by Asseraf's easygoing reassurances. After all, I knew little about diplomacy and public press conferences. But I was glad to have met him, and glad he would be there the next day.

Before I left Israel my daughter had told me, "Have some fun there, Mom! Relax, do something different."

"Like what? Do you have any suggestions?" I asked my daughter distractedly as I concentrated on packing up my papers.

"Well, Mom, why don't you have a manicure?"

I laughed. A manicure? It was out of character for me, and totally irrelevant for what I saw as my mission. I had never had a manicure, and the last time I had worn nail polish was at my own wedding.

The morning after arriving in Brussels, I turned in the direction opposite to the government buildings and tourist locations. I had had enough of monuments. I found myself weaving through a middle-class neighborhood of groceries and small businesses and narrow sidewalks. I saw boxes of glistening raspberries for sale, and luscious grapes from Spain. Even though for once I had no shopping to do, I had to resist the temptation of buying them. If I were there as a regular tourist, I know I would have bought some fruit, washed it in the sink of my hotel room, and dried it with Kleenex. As it was, I went on by.

Passing a cosmetician's shop, a sign in the window caught my eye: "Manicures, 45 minutes." Well, I said to myself, I certainly don't have forty-five minutes to spare. Then a small notice underneath caught my eye: "Nail polish application." Was this fate?

Twenty minutes later I was back out on the street with glistening nails painted a deep perfect dark crimson. The manicurist was a sweet, friendly girl who chattered away with me, as I tried to keep up in my rusty French. Where was she from? I asked. Lebanon, she answered casually. My day of coexistence had began earlier than I thought. Throughout the day my hands took me by surprise, as I saw beautiful red stranger's nails flash before my eyes.

Mini-beauty treatment aside, I must have practiced my speech under my breath fifty times during those two days as I walked the Belgian streets.

I had given thought to how I should look. For the ceremony I had chosen a black dress and matching jacket, and borrowed my mother's special pearls.

Friends back in Israel had given me all sorts of support. Shelly told me where to buy stockings for my trip, an item not in big demand in June in Israel, as the temperature holds steadily in the eighties and nineties. Paulette suggested buying two pairs and carrying the extra one in my handbag. Francoise listened to me delivering the draft of my speech; her approval meant a lot. My daughter was my guinea-pig audience, too, the day before I left. A congratulatory telegram from friends Dalia and Dan greeted me in my hotel. I arrived alone in Brussels, but full of wishes from people back in Israel.

I had been asked to meet at the offices of Common Ground, a ten-minute taxi ride away. I ordered a cab from my hotel room, and dressed in excitement.

The day of the ceremony fell on the date of the final exam of the course I taught at Tel Aviv University. A colleague replaced me at the exam and called me at my hotel room to relay the students' questions about the test paper I had put together. As luck would have it, a time issue arose, so I spent the last minutes in the hotel talking through the problem with the university.

Finally I was ready to go, to try to represent the best face of the country where I lived.

But when I got downstairs the cab was not there. That was a contingency I hadn't thought of. The last thing I wanted was to be late to what might be the one prize ceremony of my life. The reception clerk was checking a middle-aged couple into the hotel. I paced the lobby, waiting impatiently, but they talked on and on.

I interrupted, anxiously bursting out, "I have a very important appointment!" The couple looked up at me, annoyed. The clerk phoned the cab company and reassured me. Finally the taxi pulled up.

When I arrived at Common Ground, I was early after all. I was told the third recipient of the prize, French Professor Dominic Moisi, would be arriving soon with his wife; then we would all go together to the ceremony. Nusseibeh would arrive separately with the head of Common Ground, directly from meetings with public officials. I knew that Moisi was a professor at the French Institute for International Relations and I had read his article about the role Europe could play in the Mideast peace process, but that was the extent of my knowledge of him. I wondered what kind of person he would turn out to be.

A good twenty minutes later the Moisis finally walked in. Turning to meet them I found myself face to face with the couple from the hotel reception desk. The Common Ground people began a flowery introduction. But the Moisis looked at me sardonically. "We already know each other," they said. They had walked all the way to the office. I tried periodically for the rest of the evening to make conversation with Moisi and his wife, but never got past a certain frostiness.

Accompanied by officials from Common Ground, we pulled up at the modernistic imposing European Parliament, went through security, and into a wood-paneled hall.

As I entered I spotted Sari Nusseibeh standing to one side, a stream of people waiting to shake his hand and introduce themselves to him. Nusseibeh had been flown in that morning on the predawn flight from Israel and had spent a nonstop day in meetings with European leaders. By the time I saw him he looked beat, his eyes red rimmed, his clothes rumpled. Nusseibeh was the calling card of the evening, but he resembled a person who would be glad for a chance to rest.

For me the ceremony was a highlight of my writing life. For Nusseibeh it was just another of his many appearances. I was introduced to him, and he greeted me politely but without special interest.

It seemed clear that he had neither read my article nor recalled ever hearing of me.

The ceremony was held in a beautiful semicircular hall that reminded me of the United Nations chambers I had visited on guided tours for the public during my childhood in New York. Only half the seats were filled, with diplomats and the press. A camera filmed from beginning to end, I had been told Al-Jazeera Arab television was to air the proceedings.

Before the ceremony started, Chaim Assaraf spotted me and introduced me to his colleague, whom he described as the number-two man in the Jordanian embassy. With great courtesy, the Jordanian diplomat told me what a courageous person I was. I demurred, knowing that what might to others look like courage was at best naïveté.

I approached Moisi who had seated himself in one of the auditorium's seats and was scribbling down something on a piece of paper. Moisi was diminutive, reminiscent more of a mischievous leprechaun than an eminent political scientist.

"What are you writing?" I asked.

"Why, my speech!" he responded with a laugh.

The high-profile keynote speaker, Christopher Patten, exuded an air of self-confidence and empowerment. White haired and stout with a florid British complexion, Patten prefaced his remarks with greetings to his two old friends who had won the award, Nusseibeh and Moisi. The words slipped easily and tinkling from Patten's practiced lips: "Let me say straight away what a great pleasure it is to be with you this evening for this awards ceremony and, in making these awards, not simply to celebrate the work of three very distinguished and brave journalists but also to celebrate the work of the European Center for Common Ground." Then, in what seemed to me a lengthy talk, he responded to a Mideast policy speech President George W. Bush had made that week. Sitting on the podium, I was too excited to pay attention. The prize recipients were seated at a table on the podium, with Nusseibeh in the middle, flanked by myself and Moisi.

As Patten spoke, I began to hear a faint clicking beside me. At first I ignored it, but it went on, unmistakable. The noise sounded like marbles being hit against one another. It was coming from the direction of Nusseibeh. Finally, I cast a surreptitious sidelong glance. Nusseibeh's head was inclined toward Patten. Suddenly under the table I saw a flash of bright blue. And then I saw his hands working a strand of blue beads, twirling them over and over through his fingers. It was the same gesture I had seen in the Old City of Jerusalem, where Arab men in long robes crouched down on their haunches leaning against walls, and impassively running worry beads through their hands. I had heard that Nusseibeh was a heavy smoker. Maybe these beads were his pacifier. Did he need one, I wondered?

Vice president of Common Ground Susan Collin Marks, an earnest and genteel South African, made introductory remarks about the awards. She had committed her life to the dispute-resolution organization, and it was clear that the ceremony was another chance to put its agenda in the limelight. She too signaled the courage of us three recipients. At her words I jotted down an addendum to the remarks I was soon to deliver.

Moisi was the first recipient to speak. His words were informal in the extreme. Essentially his speech was a glorified thank you. He embraced Patten, and said how happy and pleased he was to receive the prize personally from his old friend.

Then it was my turn. I took my paper up to the podium. I had printed it out in fourteen-point, double-spaced, bold type, the same paper I had practiced over and over in the last day and a half in Brussels, declaiming to trees and the glances of surprised passersby.

I looked around the room at the unfamiliar faces, and then my eyes rested on the Israeli diplomat and his Jordanian colleague sitting side by side and smiling at me. The Israeli was corpulent and round, the Jordanian slight and thin; seeing them seated one next to the other gave me courage before I began: two opposites from back home sitting together, unlikely friends. I spoke for my allotted five minutes, the one policy address of my lifetime, to give a voice to people in Israel who didn't fit the stereotype of conquerors and occupiers.

Here is what I said:

"During the last black week in Israel five babies arrived at the pediatric intensive care unit in Wolfson Hospital near Tel Aviv, all of them close to death. But none were the children you read about in the headlines. All these babies were born with heart defects so severe that without surgery none would survive. This week each is going through a complicated operation. All five are Palestinian—three from Gaza and two from the West Bank. Some of them have already been to this hospital before, diagnosed in the clinic that treats Palestinian children every Tuesday. Their parents or grandparents came too, and will stay with them throughout their months in the hospital.

"They are among the 150 Palestinian children who have undergone cardiac surgery performed since 1995 by the Israeli organization Save a Child's Heart. The staff comprises both Jews and Arabs, and the babies lie in the cardiac unit among Jewish babies who, like them, are fighting for their lives.

"Neither these babies nor those who treat them ever reach the limelight. Last Tuesday morning when three of them arrived in the hospital and were rushed to be connected to oxygen, the headlines screamed of other children not too far away, children who seemed luckier because they were born with healthy hearts. But, on a simple bus ride to school, they met a brutal untimely death.

"Like many other people, I often feel overwhelmed by the endless calamities. Twenty months ago I wrote about the first child victim of this Intifada, whose Palestinian father it was my privilege to know. Now, after so much bloodletting, who can keep all the tragedies straight?

"But I want to impress upon you that in Israel now there are people who, when they talk of building walls, the walls they mean are walls between the leaking chambers of a baby's heart. The knives they wield are scalpels. Their battle plans are recovery.

"Physicians for Human Rights is another Israeli organization engaged in health care with Palestinians. The Jewish and Arab doctors in Physicians for Human Rights maintain ties with their colleagues in Palestinian hospitals. Every Saturday on their day off a volunteer team of doctors sets up a mobile clinic in West Bank villages, bringing medicines and treatment. Ten days ago, for example, six Israeli physicians—an internist, two family doctors, a surgeon, an orthopedist, and a pediatrician—arrived in the village of Deir Balout near Nablus. On that day they gave care to 370 patients and arranged follow-up treatment within Israel for nine with severe problems.

"Physicians for Human Rights and Save a Child's Heart are not alone. Despite the understandable breakdown of cooperation budding in so many fields just a few years ago, other Israelis and Palestinians continue to bravely work together. For doctors it is perhaps easier because what they do is concrete. Contacts built on words are more fragile. For people no longer believe in words.

"Still there are those of incredible courage, like the hundreds of Palestinian and Israeli parents who belong to the Bereaved Families Forum. All of them have had their own children killed by the other side. Now when they meet they must travel all the way to London, because face-to-face encounters in the Middle East are not possible today. For the rest of their lives these parents will suffer from wounded hearts no surgeon can heal. But instead of crying in dark rooms or joining the ranks of hatred, they, like the doctors, are hoping to give other children a future.

"Sometimes people even do things that in other circumstances would be considered normal. A week ago today in between the bombings a group of eighteen Palestinian and Jewish teenagers in Jerusalem put on the circus performance they had trained together for all year. After their enthusiastic show before a mixed audience, a 16-year-old Palestinian trapeze artist was asked if she could suggest any solutions to the Palestinian and Israeli leaders. Her quick and simple response: 'Maybe they should join the circus.'

"In my work I try to expose, through examples like these, that in the midst of horror and hate there is still contact and caring."

Then I spoke the words I had added while on the podium: "A lot has been said about courage here tonight. Believe me, I am far from courageous. I write what I do because I am afraid, afraid for all of us. I see trying to reach common ground as the only way out."

At that point a cell phone starting ringing in the audience. It rang three, four, five times. I forced myself to look up and smile. I stopped talking, and said jokingly, "It happens every time!" The audience laughed, relieved. It looked as if they might believe I was used to speaking before assemblies and having to deal with phones ringing, and not just mine, which usually went off as I was choosing the tomatoes at the fruit store or driving a car pool. Far up in the hall a man fumbled in his briefcase for the offending telephone, and called down in an embarrassed sheepish voice with thick Arabic accent, "Many pardons." It seemed I had carried it off, but I was upset at this interruption just as I was reaching the crescendo of my words.

"We don't hear much about hope these days," I finished off: "But if there is any hope left, these real unsung people are at its vanguard. Poet Jay Laden has written: 'Wherever there is a chasm there will also be a bridge'. We must resist despairing from the darkness of our chasm. Instead we must dedicate ourselves to the building of that bridge.

"If we will it," I ended, "it is no dream."

I wondered if anyone in the audience knew I had chosen to close with Theodor Herzl's famous words predicting the establishment of the Jewish state, words that every Israeli schoolchild knows by heart.

The Israeli diplomat might have been the only one to recognize them, if he was listening.

I returned to my seat, the clapping of the audience ringing in my ears. Was the applause long or short, perfunctory or enthusiastic? I had no idea in the flush of the moment, an excited novice. But I felt my voice had rung out strong and clear, I had not stumbled, and I had delivered the message I had wanted to the best of my ability.

Then it was Sari Nusseibeh's turn. Nusseibeh approached the microphone projecting the same modesty, almost diffidence, that I recalled from his speech in Savyon during the winter.

"I grew up in Jerusalem," began Nusseibeh. As a child he lived on the Jordanian side adjacent to the border that had run through the middle of the city since the war that followed the creation of the State of Israel in 1948. Nusseibeh would gaze at Israeli Jerusalem on the other side of the barbed wire and the no-man's-land and try to imagine the lives of the people living there.

As Nusseibeh spoke, my mind went back to my first visit to Israel with my parents in 1959, when I was 10 years old. I too had visited that part of Jerusalem, and had been stunned by the shocking yellow placards next to barbed wire with their frightening writing: "Warning! Border ahead!" I had taken photographs of those signs and still had them in my album. The only border I knew was the invisible one we crossed when going to visit our family in Canada. It occurred to me that Nusseibeh and I might have seen each other as 10-year-old children glimpsing each other across Jerusalem's no-man's-land.

My attention turned back to Nusseibeh's words. In June 1967, after Israel had won the lightning quick Six-Day War, the barbed wire abruptly came down. Israel's victory reunited the city under sole Israeli hegemony. There was suddenly nothing preventing 19-year-old Nusseibeh from crossing the chasm that had existed throughout his life. He set out from his house and walked freely across the former no-man's-land toward the Jewish houses on the other side. But just before reaching them he paused, turned around, and looked in the direction from which he had come.

"I looked at my house with new eyes, trying to imagine how a child living in the Jewish house would have been imagining me." And from this Nusseibeh turned to the point of his speech: "We have to understand Israeli society and Israelis have to understand us. We have to understand their concerns and they have to understand ours. It's true; neither society can attain the full aspiration that we would like to attain.

But surely it is possible to create life for both of us. I believe that it is far more important to create life for both of us [rather] than no life."

I was drawn once again into the eloquence of Nusseibeh's images, and had I not been sitting on the podium, might very well have wanted to write another article about him.

Then sooner than I had imagined, the speeches were over and it was time for the question session I had been dreading. I might have saved my anxiety. Out of the half dozen or so queries, not a one was directed to me. Nor to either Moisi or Nusseibeh. It was Patten alone who was asked about policy matters relating to the European Union's stance toward the Palestinian–Israeli conflict.

During the cocktail reception afterward in the adjacent hall, the tall, elegant German ambassador and his refined attaché came to shake my hand, and the smiling Jordanian diplomat appeared again to congratulate me. But other than that I was not the center of any attention. I ate peanuts, sipped Campari, and watched people clustering around Nusseibeh.

The evening was capped off by a dinner. Seven of us sat at a narrow table in a boisterous crowded local restaurant: our three hosts from Common Ground—South African Susan Collin Marks, Belgian Geoffrey Weichselbaum, and British Laura Davis—and Nusseibeh, Moisi and his wife, and me.

Relaxed by the wine, I asked Nusseibeh seated opposite me if he had been subjected to stringent security checks upon leaving Ben-Gurion airport.

"Yes and no," he smiled. "They did take me upstairs and ask me a lot of questions, though. But I understand them. In their place I would do the same." Everything Nusseibeh said, he said with a smile.

I told Nusseibeh about the recent episode I had heard of an Arab woman lawyer from Haifa who, upon leaving Israel with a delegation of the Israel Tennis Center, had had a more extreme experience. Her young daughter was one of a group of talented tennis-playing children chosen to tour the United States in a fund-raising drive for the Center. The mother, also a fund raiser for the Tennis Center, was one of the accompanying adults. The girl stood amidst the group of excited children in the airport, all wearing T-shirts with the Tennis Center logo. But then, going through security, the Arab mother and child were singled out, separated from the group, and intensively interrogated before being cleared for departure. The woman, an Israeli citizen born in Haifa into a prominent family, was insulted and incensed. She even considered filing a lawsuit against the airport security authorities. Being Arab subjected them to extra questioning; even belonging to an official Israeli delegation hadn't precluded it.

Nusseibeh listened to the story. Then he responded very simply. "Ah, yes, but that woman was an Israeli," he said wryly. "No wonder she was upset. I am a Palestinian, and that makes all the difference. I expect these things to happen to me."

Now that the ceremony was over, my appetite came back, but the food was surprisingly indifferent. Then came dessert, with everybody protesting they were too full to order. They settled on a communal order of profiteroles, along with several forks. As nothing before had done that evening, those chocolate-laced pastries created a brotherhood of happiness. Nusseibeh, Marks, Davis, Weichselbaum, and the Moisis—I watched them plunging their forks into that one plate, smiling wider smiles with every bite, and closing their eyes with pleasure.

It was a strange crew, seven strangers of different nationalities, all linked by the Middle East, sitting around one table because of it. The conversation was lively and friendly, the wine was poured frequently. Everybody told pleasant stories, congratulated one another on the successful ceremony, and toasted the Search for Common Ground.

Yet it seemed to me, as it had also during the proceedings in the European Parliament, that while everybody was doing nothing but talking about the Middle East, the Middle East was the very thing missing from that festive warm twinkling June evening in the heart of Europe.

We were enjoying ourselves and patting ourselves on the back on account of the Middle East, and all the while back home the Middle East was still suffering and sweating and bleeding from its many wounds.

I was being wined and dined in Brussels because I had written about the tragedy of Jamal al-Durrah. He could not have conceived of that table, yet for me he hung there, like a ghost.

A month or two later I received a videocassette in the mail from the Brussels office of the Search for Common Ground. It was, they said, a compilation of the Al-Jazeera footage of the award ceremony and a clip taken by an independent photographer, a memento for me. With excitement, I sat down to watch the tape with my family. First we sat through Patten's long policy speech. Then there was a short segment showing Moisi.

"Now I come," I told my husband and daughter.

There followed not more than five wordless seconds of me in my black dress and my mother's pearls walking down from the podium and smiling, and then the footage skipped to long shots of Nusseibeh accepting his plaque, Nusseibeh giving his speech, and finally Nusseibeh in a circle of Arabs, each one waiting in turn to shake his hand.

I had my award certificate on the wall, I had the wonderful experience of giving a speech that I viewed as a tribute to the great things among tragedy that still exist in the State of Israel. I had had my manicure, and my Cinderella memories of being a celebrity for one night. It was good I had gotten that disappointing video. What I saw on it made me realize my coach had turned back into the pumpkin it really was.

Chapter Eleven

Antiquity at My Doorstep

Diplomatic initiatives, high-powered negotiators, tireless emissaries, public relations support, political pressure—as far back as I remember the United States has been pushing doggedly for a solution. I've met waves of American diplomats fresh and optimistic at the start of their Israeli tour who finish up cynical and worn out.

On April 30, 2003, the United States and its diplomatic partners proposed another plan, a highly publicized timetable setting stages for "a two-state solution" leading to "the emergence of an independent, democratic, and viable Palestinian state living side by side in peace and security with Israel." This document, known as the Road Map, mandated as a first step an unequivocal statement by Palestinian leadership for an "immediate and unconditional cease-fire to end armed activity and all acts of violence against Israelis anywhere." Among Israel's corresponding duties were immediate withdrawal from Palestinian territories reoccupied during the Intifada and cessation of violence against civilians.

Palestinians and Israelis gave the Road Map their typical de facto welcome. The very day it was published, a suicide bomber attacked Mike's Place, an Israeli jazz club next to the American Embassy in Tel Aviv, killing three and wounding over sixty. The following day the Israelis struck inside Gaza, killing sixteen Palestinians including a 2-year-old toddler, two 13-year-old boys, and a 67-year-old man. This seemingly endless reiteration of incident–retaliation–incident–retaliation is more than numbing. It approaches a travesty that is unspeakable but true: death has become so commonplace as to be boring.

The Israeli government claims its operations are retaliations aimed only at militants, that it targets suspected terrorists and that all other civilian casualties are unintended. The official Palestinian leadership pays lip service to being against terrorism and claims it cannot control extremist factions, such organizations as the Al-Aksa Brigade and Hamas. There are truth and falsehood to both assertions. If there were no Palestinian uprising, there would be no Israeli planes bombing refugee camps, no razing of groves, no targeted assassinations. Yet the number of Palestinian infants, elderly, and infirm killed belies Israeli carefulness, if not good faith. Similarly, Palestinian extremists are perhaps uncontrollable by the Palestinian Authority, but its officials have done far less than their utmost to try to curb them, and may even have been implicated. Furthermore, suicide bombers are glorified and their families honored.

Whatever may be the analyses—the verdicts of political scientists, apologists, pundits, diplomats, foreign correspondents—I am resigned to one incontrovertible conclusion. Despite the rhetoric of Israeli and Palestinian holders of power, there is one nonideological priority too low on everyone's agenda: saving human life.

If the motto "saving human life" occupied first, second, or even fifth place in the respective policies, there would be a lot fewer fresh graves and a lot fewer broken hearts. Would it be too much to ask that each side start every meeting, every memo, every policy decision by saying: "What does this accomplish to save human life?" To my own criticism that this sounds simplistic, I respond that it is not simplistic, but simple. And the simple is often what has been obfuscated. If the mind-set could be changed to that wavelength, perhaps inhabitants of the Middle East would cease living by their ancient and enduring motto of outmoded harshness: An eye for an eye, a tooth for a tooth.

Those of us who have been here for the duration are resigned to taking new peace initiatives not with a grain of salt, but with a ton. Luckily, salt is one of Israel's few natural resources. Around the Dead Sea, where in the Bible God turned Lot's disobedient wife into a pillar of salt, salts are still extracted from the ground. They are used for chemical industries and marketed around the world for cosmetic purposes. Unlike precious water, salt abounds. The two sides are adept at rubbing it into each other's wounds, with plenty left over for those of us who have with time moved from hope to skepticism.

During the tense days preceding the Iraq war of 2003, the attention of the world was focused on Washington and Iraq. But besides worries about gas masks and possible missile attacks, for the Israeli–Palestinian conflict it was business as usual.

The casualties suffered in one arbitrary week, from March 9 to March 16, 2003, are a good example of how the lethal dynamic in the Middle East proceeds on its well-oiled routine. It began with the funeral of one Christian American girl and ended with the killing of another.

On Sunday, March 9, 14-year-old Abigail Little was buried in the Christian part of the Haifa cemetery. She was eulogized by the American Ambassador in Israel, Daniel Kurtzer, and by her father, a minister at the Baptist church in Haifa. Born in New Hampshire, Abigail had lived in Israel for thirteen of her fourteen years. Unlike the children of most Christian Americans who are sent to schools for foreigners, Abigail and her three siblings attended regular public schools. Abigail had been riding the bus after school the previous Wednesday when a suicide bomber blew himself up, killing her and fifteen others. Two other pupils at Abigail's high school died as well, 16-year-old Daniel Harush and 13-year-old Yuval Medelevitch. Yuval and Abigail had participated together in "Children Teaching Children," a school program aimed at encouraging understanding between Jewish and Arab students. Her casket was draped with both the American and Israeli flags, and mourners in the hundreds sang "Amazing Grace" in English and Hebrew. Also buried that day were two settlers who lived in the West Bank Jewish settlement of Kiryat Arba near Hebron; Palestinian gunmen had burst upon the couple sitting at their Sabbath meal and opened fire.

On Monday, March 10, a 20-year-old Israeli soldier guarding the road used by settlers to travel to the Tomb of the Patriarchs in Hebron was killed in an ambush by a Palestinian sniper. The Popular Front for the Liberation of Palestine and Hamas took credit for the attack.

On Tuesday, March 11, the sniper in Monday's killing, who took refuge in a nearby apartment building, was killed when the Israeli army hunted him down. In southern Gaza that same night, Israeli soldiers killed two Palestinians after noticing them digging near the fence surrounding a Jewish settlement. Fourteen pipe bombs were found beside their bodies. Also on Tuesday 19-year-old Moran Shoshan, who had been injured on the bus with Abigail, died of her wounds, raising the fatality count to seventeen. It was unusual for her to have been there, for Moran's boyfriend had been afraid of her taking buses and had tried to drive her whenever possible. Moran's mother said, "Her [high school matriculation] mark was 98. Nobody is perfect, but she was almost perfect."

On Wednesday, March 12, Israeli troops, looking for militants in the West Bank village of Saida, rounded up all the village men for questioning. Other Palestinians on the village outskirts opened fire on the soldiers. One soldier was killed, and in the resulting chase soldiers killed a member of the Islamic Jihad.

A car riddled with bullets was pictured on page one on Thursday, March 13, beside reports of the deaths of two Israelis in their early twenties. Both had been working as security guards in the West Bank. But Palestinians had not killed them. Israelis were stunned to hear the two men were felled by friendly fire, mistaken by Israeli troops for Palestinian militants. Commentator Amos Harel observed in *Haaretz*: "Had yesterday's incident . . . ended with the death of two Palestinians, the story would probably not have merited more than a few lines in this morning's papers. Incidents in which Israeli Defense Forces troops accidentally shoot the wrong man are hardly rare in the territories." In another part of the West Bank four Palestinians who opened fire on an Israeli patrol were killed by Israeli soldiers.

On Friday, March 14, Israeli troops attacked a hideout of the extremist Palestinian group Islamic Jihad in Jenin. In the shootout six Jihad men were killed. On the West Bank two Palestinians suspected of collaborating with Israel were executed by the Palestinian group Al-Aksa Martyrs Brigades.

On Saturday, March 15, there were no fatalities. As Yesheskel Lein, researcher for the human rights information center B'Tselem said wryly, "There are also some days when nobody is killed."

The week wound up on Sunday with Israel causing itself one of the most damaging incidents of the Intifada. Rachel Corrie was a 23-year-old American college student who came to the Rafah refugee camp in Gaza as part of the pro-Palestinian International Solidarity Movement. The Israeli army, believing that ammunition was being smuggled into Gaza from nearby Egypt via houses near the border, was engaged in demolishing the houses using a Caterpillar bulldozer. On March 16 Corrie was acting as a human shield, standing in front of the bulldozer to prevent its advance. As it approached she dropped to her knees, either as a deliberate gesture or because she lost her footing. The bulldozer did not stop. It ran Corrie over, and she died shortly thereafter.

At the time of her death Corrie was wearing a bright orange jacket. Her fellow volunteers were adamant that the driver couldn't have missed seeing her. But an Israeli army investigation concluded that because of the angle of vision and blind spots in the line of view, the driver had not noticed Corrie. It nevertheless ordered TV monitors installed in bulldozer cabins to compensate for blind spots in the future. The Israeli version was met with skepticism, and the incident caused international outrage.

Whatever sympathy Israel had gained by the slaughter of Abigail Little was wiped out by the shocking death of Rachel Corrie. With her face in newspapers and on posters, Corrie became a martyr. Abigail Little's murder faded into oblivion.

Despite its daily body counts, the second week of March 2003 was not an exceptionally bad one as the Intifada went. All the victims were grist for the mill of the relentless Situation.

A year later, the Situation had not improved. Bodies littered the "Road Map" announced in 2003, and people questioned whether both Oslo and the Road Map were dead. During the same week one year later, March 9 to 16, 2004, twenty-five people were killed as a direct result of the conflict, fifteen of them Palestinians and ten Israelis.

I was reminded of the anniversary of Rachel Corrie's death when I came upon a bitter article written by her cousin Elizabeth Corrie in the *International Herald Tribune*. She complained that the American government had not investigated the death and said Americans should question "how it is that an unarmed U.S. citizen can be killed with impunity by a soldier from an allied nation receiving massive U.S. aid, using a product manufactured in the United States by a U.S corporation and paid for with U.S. tax dollars."

Unlike Rachel Corrie, whose anniversary saw events across the United States, American victim Abigail Little's first year anniversary passed in silence. Why was her murder less horrific a crime than Rachel Corrie's? I asked myself. Why do thousands know Rachel's name and not Abigail's?

Sitting with my daughter in front of our television in the spring of that one year anniversary, I watched an Israeli documentary movie in which Abigail's mother, Heidi Little, held up a photo of her daughter and talked of her memories. This heartbreaking Israeli film, *Lullaby*, directed by Adi Arbel, showed Little and ten more women whose children had been killed during the Intifada—four Palestinians and six Israelis. Most had given birth to subsequent children, but theirs was a void that could not be filled. They addressed the camera with tragic faces, reliving their loss, while their "replacement" toddlers tugged for attention. One Palestinian mother folded and unfolded the brown corduroy pants and striped T-shirt her little boy had worn, stroking them on her lap. An Israeli mother who had lost her toddler and had since had another son dressed the new baby in his older brother's clothes she saved; often she couldn't wait to put him in outfits that were still too large.

In Arabic the term *father of girls* conveys a mix of sympathy and ridicule. Likewise, the daily morning prayer of Jewish males commands them to thank God they were not born a woman.

But in Israel today the tables have turned 180 degrees. Having daughters, not sons, is the biggest blessing here. For female Israeli soldiers usually don't risk being shot at, nor are they required to do the shooting.

In 1997 almost three years before the formal start of the Intifada, wedged between the news items on the radio, I heard announced the death of 8-year-old Palestinian Ali Jawarish. Ali was shot in the forehead by an Israeli soldier as he stood among a group of children in Bethlehem watching the stones and fire being exchanged there; four days later he died in a hospital.

Hearing the news, I wanted to become again the mother of an 8-year-old child, at least for a moment. So I went over to the albums where I had pasted my own children's photographs, arranged year by year on the bookshelf. I pulled down three, flipping the pages until I found the class photo of each of my daughters in Israeli third grade. That's the grade Ali Jawarish would be finishing, were he still alive.

I looked from face to face on the class photo of my youngest daughter's third-grade class. I visualized any of her classmates lying, head bandage soaked with blood, resembling the last image of Ali that had been plastered over the newspapers.

It might have been the child kneeling on wobbly knees in the front line of the class photo, or the one standing right next to mine. Or the one from down the block, had he had the misfortune to live not on our orderly tree-lined street, but on another one not too far away in this same tortured Middle East.

That other street would be a street like the one we saw on the TV news, a street without sidewalks or bicycle lanes or school crossing guards, like the turbulent road with burning tires and live ammunition where Ali had been standing.

Every mother who loses a child undergoes her own unending catastrophe, a catastrophe that stretches into desolate perpetuity. Every parent who has sat numbly beneath garish fluorescent lights keeping a nighttime vigil over a hospitalized child knows how much bitterness would have been added to his anguish, if instead of a fault of nature that struck his child, it had been, as in Ali's case, the deadly forces of man.

On the very night Ali died, his bereaved parents donated their son's organs to save other children. "They're for whoever needs them," Ali's father said. "For Arab or for Jew." The next day Ali Jawarish's heart, lungs, and kidneys were sewn into the bodies of terminally ill children on the transplant waiting list. A parallel heartbreaking transcendence over hatred was repeated when the parents of Scottish Jewish tourist Yonatan Gladstone, killed in a 2002 Tel Aviv bus bombing, donated his organs without putting any restrictions on the recipient. Now part of Yonatan lives on in a Palestinian girl who received his kidney and calls him "her brother."

I turned my glance to the third-grade class photos of my older daughters, knowing that the children in those fading images of the 1980s had reached army reserve age.

As I looked from the face of one little boy to another—this one smiling a crooked smile, that one blinking in the sunlight, a third with a serious stare—I imagined that any of them might have grown up to be the soldier who fired the bullet that lodged in Ali's brain.

To be that soldier, to be put in that moral dilemma, and then to live with the consequences of the choice forever seems its own brand of living hell. The casualties are many: the children shot, the soldiers who shoot, and the parents of them both.

I then, for one, am thankful, thankful for being a mother of girls.

Margaret Kikos was not as lucky. She lost her soldier son Beni in a roadblock ambush in 2002. Then, like the other mothers in *Lullaby*, Kikos decided to replace her lost child and become pregnant following Beni's death. There was one difference. The other mothers were young, and all the children they lost were under five. Kikos was in her fifties and only managed to conceive via fertilization treatments. When she gave birth to twins, she was 54.

I am bone tired of this conflict. Everyone around me is bone tired of this conflict. The world is bone tired of this conflict. Yet sometimes a small scenario in the midst of it all brings optimism.

Not long ago our street was repaved by the municipality and new sidewalks were put in. The job took months and turned our street into a dirt road full of potholes and bumps. Then, just as it was nearing completion and the new asphalt was about to be poured, everything came to a sudden halt.

Leaving my driveway I saw why. Directly across the narrow street from my house there stood an open ditch that hadn't been there the day before. A few yards farther on stood another one. They were encircled with ropes, and draped along the ropes were red, white, and black signs with big lettering: "Danger, Entry Forbidden. Archaeological Excavation in Progress. Israel Antiquities Authority."

I pulled my car over and approached a group of three men standing inside the ditch, digging. All were Arabs.

"What's all this?" I asked with wonder.

The men smiled, leaned on their shovels, and said, "Talk to Edna, the archaeologist," motioning toward a young woman a few yards away.

"Where are you all from?" I asked.

Uhm el Fahm, they told me, a major Israeli-Arab town.

Edna Ayash, a woman of about 30 with a floppy canvas hat covering her dark hair, was leaning over her car, and when I introduced myself, she was more than happy to share her elation.

The construction crews in the midst of their work had uncovered what looked like a piece of ancient pottery. By law, that meant that all construction had to be immediately halted and the Antiquities Authority called in. Only after they had a chance to excavate and give the all-clear signal would road building be able to resume.

"We believe we have found a burial site from the Late Bronze Age," Edna said.

"When does that date from?" I asked.

"About 1750 B.C.," Edna answered. "We found some unbelievable pieces here today. Here, I'll show you." Edna sounded like a little girl who had just been handed the most beautiful toy in the world.

She reached into her car trunk and pulled out a tiny perfect vial, no more than two inches tall. "We think this might have been a perfume container."

And then she carefully unwrapped a cloth to show me two small metal disks. "These might have been some kind of jewelry, maybe earrings."

Edna's eyes were shining. It wasn't every day that treasures surfaced.

"The Arab workers there are doing the actual excavating?" I asked. "Do they have any special training?"

"No," answered Edna. "But they have worked with us so long they know the job better than we do."

Ah, I thought to myself. As exceptional as this seems, look how things are set up. There are the unskilled manual laborers, the Arabs. And there is the university educated boss, a Jew.

Edna and her crew worked in front of my house daily for two weeks. Every day the ditch got deeper. Soon it was a hole over six feet deep. Every day I would stop to see what was new.

And almost every time Edna would show me more. The site yielded a trove of riches. Evidence was found of life during the Iron Age as well, between 1000 and 800 B.C. Israeli soil is rich in evidence from the successive civilizations that lived here in previous ages. What was exciting to the archaeologists in this find was the exceptional quality of the artifacts.

Meanwhile, other neighbors had been complaining. They were impatient. The archaeological delay was holding up the new road. The neighbors were worried about their shock absorbers. As far as I was concerned, I would have been glad to see the dig go on forever.

When I was a child summering on Long Island my cousins and I used to dig in the dirt of our suburban gardens, half hoping to uncover Indian flints like those we had read about in adventure books. Other than that, my Manhattan existence was purely a late twentieth century one of apartment buildings and concrete. When Con Edison blasted open an avenue, putting up barricades with signs that said, "Dig we must for a better New York," I imagined they might come across an old subway token or a crushed beer can.

But a perfume vial and jewelry preserved for thirty-eight centuries? I had to move to Israel to see that.

Every day I watched the past being unearthed before my eyes in front of my own driveway. Human bones were uncovered next to a big burial urn dating from the Byzantine period. Had it been the body of an Arab? Of a Jew?

Then one morning Edna said to me, "Meet my boss." He had come to check on the progress of the local team.

Edna is the archaeologist in charge of the greater Tel Aviv area. Her boss is head of the entire Mediterranean coast from the borders with Lebanon in the north to the Gaza Strip in the south, encompassing the ancient cities of Caesarea, Dor, Jaffa, and Ashkelon. Archaeologists' paradises, every one.

I approached a tall, serious man, not as young as Edna, but still seemingly in his thirties. When Edna introduced us, she told me her boss's name: Radwan Badici. I realized that the chief archaeologist of the State of Israel for the coastal region was an Arab. True, Edna was in charge of Arab laborers. But Edna's superior was himself an Arab.

All of this was going on during the months of March and April 2002, perhaps the blackest, most lethal time of the Intifada, if any period can claim that dubious honor. Palestinians and Israelis were aiming at each other's heads and pulling triggers with intent to kill. And all that time, as if nothing in the world was more pressing or of more interest than the Late Bronze Age, in front of my home there were Arabs and Jews working side by side with shovels, and then with more delicate instruments, gently brushing aside the earth and jointly exclaiming over each new find.

It has been said that archaeology is the favorite Israeli hobby. The country has been the crossroads of civilizations from pre-Biblical times through today. The Phoenicians, the Canaanites, the Hebrews, the Greeks, the Romans, the Byzantines, the Mamaluks, the Crusaders, the Ottomans—all traversed or lived on the same soil where today we go to the movies, plant flowers, get our hair cut and our cars serviced. But none of that knowledge ever created the same thrill as when I saw the evidence literally upon my doorstep.

As incredible as the ancient discoveries was the off-the-cuff relaxed cooperation, the laid-back, friendly interaction between all ranks of the archaeological service. I could not reconcile the paradox between what met me outside my home every morning and the carnage that the news on my car radio reported with comprehensive grimness.

Those are the images of Israel that I would like to carry inside me, and that I wish would be one of its defining symbols for the world.

There are millions of voiceless people of goodwill behind the painful headlines. One is a construction worker from Gaza to whom life brought tragedy. And one, perhaps, is an American woman whose house he built, who learned with time to empathize with tragedy. The accursed situation was created by human beings. All of us inherited it. It can only continue to plague us if we acquiesce.

June, 2004